REVELATION IN CHRIST

By the same author

ECUMENISM AND CATHOLICITY

Revelation in Christ

WILLIAM NICHOLLS

Chaplain to Anglican Students in Edinburgh

SCM PRESS LTD
56 BLOOMSBURY STREET
LONDON

First published 1958

©

Student Christian Movement Press
1958

Printed in Great Britain by
The Camelot Press Ltd., London and Southampton

Contents

Preface

THE foundation of Christian theology, as well as of all other forms of the spiritual life of Christians, is the conviction that God has revealed himself to man. For the greater part of the history of the Church, Christians have assumed that this revelation could be more or less identified with the Bible. Whether or not the Bible needed to be interpreted or even to be supplemented by allied sources of truth, it was itself the Word of God, or even the words of God. Since the nineteenth century the situation has altered. Biblical critics have claimed the right to read the Bible as if it were any other book, and to apply to it the same standards of literary and historical criticism and interpretation as they would to any other ancient document. The fruitfulness of this method of studying the Bible has won for it a prestige which has placed it beyond serious challenge, except in circles which are outside the main stream of the life of the Church.

Whatever its fruitfulness, the critical method of reading the Bible, now so widely adopted by theologians and even by the instructed laity, has had the consequence that those who use it find it impossible to think of the Bible as the Word of God in the same simple and unqualified sense in which their predecessors in the Church so regarded it. If the Bible is still to be believed in as the Word of God, it must be in some different sense from that implied by the old idea of verbal inspiration. Present-day Christians therefore tend to suffer from a fundamental uncertainty about the basis of their faith, and when they defend it in discussion with those who do not share it, frequently do so on grounds that have little to do with the revelation that is its actual foundation. The laity, and that section of the clergy which is chronically suspicious of the disturbing questions of the theologians, are thus peculiarly vulnerable to

7

forces in the Church which desire to bring it back from the course it has been following in these matters to a fundamentalism more rigid than the simpler pre-critical faith in the Bible as the Word of God. Others, unwilling to embrace the obscurantism of the fundamentalists, or to ignore their doubts, instead give them free and uninformed rein, substituting rationalist moralism for the Biblical faith, while retaining the name of Christian.

For the theologian, however—and unfortunately the laity is not generally in a position to be intimately aware of this—the Bible has recovered much of its former authority. But it has done so in the context of a reconsidered view of revelation, and the authority which theologians now recognize in the Bible is of a different sort from before the critical revolution. The 'biblical theologians' of today go further than their predecessors in endeavouring to exclude from their theology outlooks, attitudes and linguistic usages derived from sources outside the Bible; they are far more aware than the theologians of the pre-critical age, and indeed than the modern fundamentalists, of what is distinctive in Biblical thought, and for them biblical thought has no less authority. If they do not treat the Bible as revelation itself, in such a way that every text is equally and in the same sense the Word of God, they certainly regard it as intimately bound up with God's whole work of revelation. Their attitude is one of critical faith: they are not concerned, as the fundamentalists charge, to criticize what God has said, but, in faith that God has spoken, to use the critical powers with which he has endowed them in order to make what he has said stand out more clearly from the thoughts of men.

Nevertheless, it must be admitted that the 'biblical theologians' have not always succeeded in making clear, even to themselves, what they mean by their new, non-fundamentalist view of revelation, and they have certainly failed to make it clear to the wider public that is in one way or another interested in theological questions. Even the theological student, who begins the academic study of theology at one of our great universities, where he finds the critical method pre-supposed or

PREFACE

even axiomatic, may not find it at all easy to discover where the
locus of authority lies for those who are teaching him about
the Bible. It is not easy to point such a student to any particular
book in which he will find set out the view of revelation with
which his preceptors are working, and if he wishes to pursue
an enquiry into these matters for himself, he will find it a
lengthy task, and one which may well prove a distraction from
his proper studies, even if he is successful in the end in finding
a satisfactory position for himself.

In fact, most present-day theologians, especially if they are,
in the term that we have used, 'biblical theologians', have a
view of revelation, which satisfies their own needs, even if the
pressure of other studies has prevented them from working it
out in full. As far as theologians are concerned, there is probably little need for a new book to be written to explain what
kind of view of revelation is tenable today. The fundamental
work has already been done by a succession of thinkers of
several different churches and schools of thought, and the
result is a view of revelation which is at once more intellectually satisfying, and in the best sense of the word, more orthodox, than the old pre-critical one. Its essence lies in the shifting
of the locus of revelation from literature to history, and from
the propositional to the personal. Our great gain is that we
have recovered the primitive understanding of the Church that
Jesus Christ is himself the Word of God, and that he cannot
yield this position to anything else, even the Bible. Accordingly
the Bible regains its proper authority, not as revelation in its
own right, but as an authoritative, perhaps even an inspired,
book about Jesus Christ. For basic statements such as these
there would be a very wide measure of support amongst
present-day theologians.

A fully worked-out view of revelation on this basis is less
easy to come by. Such a dogmatics of revelation is accessible to
the specialist, though not perhaps, even for him, in a very
assimilable form, in the writings of more than one continental
theologian, and in a somewhat different and slighter form in
articles or books on other subjects, by a number of British

9

theologians. Moreover, it seems that the new view of revelation raises problems which have not always been sufficiently faced by these writers to meet our full need, either because as continentals they live in a different philosophical climate from ourselves, or because some of the problems in which we are interested did not lie within the scope of their work. The present book is an attempt to meet some of the remaining needs. In all probability it will have little to say to the professional theologian who is able to read for himself the works to which I have referred, though if any such persons do me the honour of reading this book I hope they will find it not without interest, and not less rigorously thought out, if less technical in treatment, than the books they are accustomed to read. However, this study is designedly free from the apparatus of scholarship which is appropriate to the discourse of theologians amongst themselves. It seeks to reduce both technical terminology and footnotes to manageable proportions for the lay reader.

My book is in fact intended for readers of several different kinds. One section of persons whom I have tried to help is newcomers to the study of theology, who wish to satisfy themselves about the basis of their study, though it will lie largely in the historical field once it gets under way. A second group might consist of instructed laity, who care enough about the subject to be willing to follow a closely reasoned and not always easy argument, provided it is reasonably free from undefined technical terminology. A third group, which is likely to include many clergy, consists of those who like myself are concerned to examine the fundamental basis of the mission of the Church, whether at home or abroad, in the world of the twentieth century. It would give great pleasure to the author if this study also found readers amongst that small number of agnostics, especially those who are somewhat philosophically minded, who think it important to go on discussing with Christians the basis of their faith.

The plan of this book is governed by theological considerations, and for this reason some readers may find it helpful to re-read the first four chapters after they have read the last three. But the order of the chapters is that of the argument of the book. We cannot discuss the rationality of revelation and its relationship to human thought unless a revelation has actually occurred. Accordingly the book does not begin with a discussion of the possibility or the necessity of revelation, but, after a brief survey of the field in which revelation intervenes, with an account of the revelation in Christ, from the point of view of a believer, and therefore in theological terms, even if not in technical ones. This section of the book comprises the chapters on 'The Word of God', 'God Reveals Himself' and 'The People of the Revelation'. Since it is written, like all theology, as part of the testimony of the believing Church to the act of God it does not pause to argue, but, as some might wish to put it, 'asserts' the faith of the Church. This part of the book is more closely related to prayer than to apologetic discussion.

In the last three chapters, however, those dealing with 'The Knowledge of God', 'The Expression of Revelation in Thought' and 'The Revelation of God the Creator', the viewpoint shifts somewhat, and the subject is surveyed from a position more nearly alongside the modern agnostic. Without abandoning the general standpoint of the book, which is, broadly, empirical, rather than speculative, this section endeavours to relate revelation and its correlative, the knowledge of God, to human thought and culture, and even to the difficulties of contemporary people in believing. At the same time, it is precisely in these chapters that the writer is aware of probing a little beyond the well-established positions of a present-day theology of revelation to ask newer questions. Though I am by no means the first to ask these questions or to attempt to answer them, it is in these chapters that any personal contribution I have to make must be sought.

At this point it may be asked what position I occupy in the debate between different schools of thought in these matters. I find it difficult to suppose that my outlook on revelation could be accurately aligned with that of any of the present-day groupings of theologians. I am obviously neither a modernist nor a fundamentalist, nor yet a Bultmannite. I am equally obviously at one with many theologians today in endeavouring to set forth a consistently Christological view of revelation. One consequence of my own understanding of the implications of this is that I may seem to some Protestants to say too little about the Bible and too much about the Church, while I may seem to some Catholics to say too little about the formulated doctrinal teaching of the Church in favour of a more 'personalistic' understanding of the knowledge of God. On the other hand, I do not follow the more uncompromising continental adherents of the Christological view of revelation in supposing that the prime duty of the Church to believe in and bear witness to the actual revelation of God in Christ precludes apologetic discussion as a means of clearing the way for recognizing the revelation itself, and of making faith a live issue. In fact, and this is important to my own understanding of the matter, such discussion does not come at the beginning of the book but towards the end, following the theological plan of the book. The purpose of the book is certainly not primarily apologetic; it will be recalled that one of its principal aims is to be of use to beginners in theology.

Finally, I hope that no one who is interested in the subject matter of this book will derive any impression that I occupy some special position of my own outside the main stream of Christian thought at this period in the Church's life. It is, I believe, not unconnected with the fact that this book is the work of an Anglican that it seeks to occupy a reconciling position in the current discussion. It is intended, indeed, to make available to a wider audience conclusions already widely accepted amongst theologians themselves, though I naturally present them in a form which is convincing to myself. I have conceived my task as one of clarification, not innovation, since I write as one occupying a pastoral charge, and not as a professional theologian. The impulse to write this book originated from the memory of my own struggles to understand revelation when I myself began the study of theology, and also from the conviction, which I should be glad to find a mistaken one, that no other book existed which fulfilled the functions I had in mind. Since I began to write the subject of revelation has begun again to receive the attention of theologians, and at least two books have appeared whose purposes are complementary to those of the present volume. None the less, although I have avoided consulting them while the book was in preparation, in order not to confuse my own thought during the crucial stage of writing, my impression now is that both Dr Baillie's *The Idea of Revelation in Recent Thought* and W. J. Wolf's *Man's Knowledge of God*, though written from a point of view broadly similar to my own, cover somewhat different ground, and in particular do not enter in such detail into the questions discussed in the three final chapters of the present work.

Finally, I should like to thank my wife and Professor D. M. MacKinnon, Mr Alasdair MacIntyre and the Rev. James and Mrs Nansie Blackie for reading and commenting on the manuscript of this book. While the reader must not suppose that these friendly critics are necessarily in agreement with the argument of this book, its presentation would have been notably more obscure and faulty if their help had not been forthcoming.

Anglican Students' Chaplaincy   WILLIAM NICHOLLS
Edinburgh
January 1957

I

God the Unknown

THE purpose of this book is to make clear what is meant and implied by the testimony of Christian faith that God has revealed himself in Jesus Christ. One of the most important, and to many, unwelcome, of these implications is that it was necessary for God to make himself known in Jesus Christ, since apart from him we do not know God. It is possible that this implication can be minimized by the suggestion that we can have a fragmentary or incomplete knowledge of God apart from Jesus Christ: but even if it can be minimized, and this remains only a possibility, which we may see cause to reject, it cannot be eliminated without eliminating what makes Christian faith Christian. It is characteristic of Christian faith to claim uniqueness, to claim the true knowledge of God, and so, to claim that God may not be truly known in other ways than through Jesus Christ.

This claim of Christian faith would be merely arrogant if it rested upon man's spiritual achievements: we have no reason to believe, and good reason to doubt, that the spiritual insights of the men of the Judaeo-Christian tradition are superior to those of Hindu, Buddhist, Moslem or even atheist thinkers. In fact it rests upon something else: upon the belief that in Jesus Christ God *revealed* himself to the world, uniquely and sufficiently, and so finally. Revelation, therefore, rightly understood, comes close to being the distinctive element in Christianity, for it cannot be separated from God's act of reconciling the world to himself in Christ, of restoring sinful man to the knowledge and love of himself.

When we survey the world of ideas about God outside the circle illuminated by Jesus Christ, what alternatives do we see to the revelation of God in Christ? We see in the first place the religions of the world, great and small, high and low.

Secondly, we see, less prominent today than in the past, but looming large in the history of philosophy, metaphysical theism in its various forms. Thirdly, there is its obverse, atheism. Lastly, and in the Western world this is perhaps the most commonly held view of God, there is the view that the question is not important. God may exist, even probably exists, but it doesn't matter. He cannot be known, except perhaps by a few spiritually gifted people, and in any case it doesn't make any difference to life as we know it.

When we look at this field, surely we are struck by the variety rather, than the sameness, of the picture. The men of the middle ages used to offer as one of the arguments for the existence of God an *argumentum ex consensu gentium*, from the agreement of mankind that there is a God. This argument must have seemed very convincing when it was first offered, for Christian thought in the high middle ages was carried on in a culture to which Christian, Jew and Moslem all contributed, and these had in common the belief that there is one God. But the argument seems less persuasive now, when we are aware that in the West only a minority are explicit and self-conscious believers in God, while elsewhere there are as many different ideas of God as there are religions. For the great religions are indeed very different from one another, and perhaps most of all in their doctrine of God.

Moreover, some of those whom we most respect intellectually, the scientists upon whose work so much of our present culture is founded, are known to be agnostics or atheists. The idea of God is certainly not self-evident to the Western mind today, nor can atheism be regarded as intellectually disreputable. Again, metaphysical theism is under attack in the philosophical world from the exponents of that philosophy which most clearly reflects the temper of mind of a scientific age. Critical philosophy from Kant onwards has revealed such flaws in the arguments that purported to demonstrate God's existence that it is doubtful if they can ever again receive wide acceptance, while logical positivism has tried to show that the claim that God exists is without meaning.

In short, some believe, others don't, but the believers do so 'on faith', as we suppose, and have no rational way of commending their faith to others, and in any case differ greatly among themselves. Such is the conclusion of most ordinary people who think from time to time about the question of God. If they leave out revelation, they are right to reach the conclusions they do. The multiplicity of man's religious ideas makes it seem *a priori* unlikely that they are well founded, and the prevalence of unbelief amongst intelligent and decent-living people makes it impossible to use the argument that everyone must have religion, and so there must be in man a need for God which only a religion can satisfy. If such a need for God exists, it must lie at so deep a level that something like a revelation would be necessary to uncover it. More and more people are dispensing with religion altogether, as something outgrown.[1] It is fair to conclude from the variety of man's religious ideas that if a true knowledge of God exists, it is hard to come by.

Very many people leave the question here. The Christian cannot do so, but must make clear, in the first place to himself, and if they will listen, to others also, the true ground of his own faith. He must decide whether it is proper to range his faith with that of the adherents of the great religions, with the metaphysical theists, or even with the agnostics, atheists and positivists, as some in effect do today. And so he must subject these positions to an examination of his own, to see whether any of them yield the knowledge of God. Does religion give us the knowledge of God? Is there, hidden amongst and beneath the diverse practices and teachings of the great religions of the world, some common factor of faith in God which could be taken as clear evidence that man can if he will know God?

The striking cultural achievements of the great religions of the world must cause us to hold them all in great respect, and

---

[1] What is said above is said in conscious disagreement with the attempts of Billy Graham and others to present the Gospel as the answer to man's religious needs, and I would hold that it remains valid in spite of statistics of a 'return to religion'.

the similarity of the roles they have played in the cultures of which they are the binding force creates a natural presupposition that they have something fundamental in common. Hinduism, Buddhism and Confucianism have doubtless been the most important factors in the making of the cultures of India and China. More strikingly still, Islam has dominated the thought and culture, as well as the spiritual lives, of millions of diverse people, and has created a unity between them which outweighs other forces however strong, as may be seen in the unity between a Pakistani and an Egyptian, as well as in the difference between a Pakistani and an Indian. It is not difficult to make Christianity appear as a member of the same series, as the binding force of what we call Western civilization. When so regarded, Christianity naturally appears as the religion of European man, paradoxically enough in view of the Palestinian origins of Christianity, and of the debts of Europe to the non-Christian civilizations of Greece and Rome.

In this light it is quite easy to see something which we can suppose all these religions, including Christianity, have in common. All teach belief in God, or at least in a Higher Power, unless it is indeed, as may well be the case, a correct understanding of early Buddhism to regard it as non-theistic. In any case, Buddhism soon acquired a theistic element. Similarly, all, at least in their more intellectual and enlightened forms (since it might be almost as awkward for Christianity as for Hinduism to be judged by its most 'popular' and debased manifestations), may be said to teach a high standard of ethical conduct. All produce saintly individuals; for pragmatic Western man, even for Christian man, this nearly settles the question; did not our Lord himself say, 'By their fruits ye shall know them'?

Thus Aldous Huxley and his followers have seen as the underlying unity of all the higher religions a 'perennial philosophy'—an interesting re-application of a term from Christian history. This perennial philosophy is considered to be essentially the same in all religions whatever its outward clothing, a mysticism of detachment and union with the divine, transcending all doctrinal differences. The doctrinal differences exist, however, and it is possible to claim that they are more obvious to the enquirer with no axe to grind than the presence of the alleged perennial philosophy. If indeed some such mystical religion is to be found among the adherents of each of these great religions, there is nothing which compels us to view it as their essential common factor. Apart from its attractiveness to ourselves, we might with equal plausibility represent it as the great heresy which menaces all, and has nearly swallowed up Hinduism. Nor is this mystical element, granted that it is to be discerned as an element in all these religions, itself a unity. Closer examination of the phenomena loosely called mysticism will reveal profound and important differences, e.g. between nature mysticism, oriental monistic mysticism and Christian and Sufi transcendental mysticism.[1]

What common residuum of teaching is left when the differences between the great religions have been excluded? Have they in fact anything at all genuinely in common, except that religion is worth while? They do not even teach with unanimity that there is one God, for some forms of Hinduism are polytheistic, while a form of Buddhism which has some claim to represent an authentic strain appears not to teach belief in God at all. Even supposing it to be a correct interpretation of the consensus of the higher religions that there is only one God, they differ strikingly in their conception of what he is like. Islam lays greatest stress upon his transcendent unity, and upon his will by which all events are predestined, though that will is understood as benevolent. The oriental religions seem to have in common a view of God as immanent in the world, as a uniform spiritual principle running through men and things, in which all differences are ultimately merged, and in which the individual may in the end find peace and joy in the renunciation of all that fosters the illusion of his individuality.

But even these apparently opposite conceptions have something in common against most forms of Christianity in the

[1] This way of classifying the differences is derived from a broadcast talk by R. C. Zaehner.

conviction that all that happens is to be accepted with resignation, whether because God wills whatever is, or because action keeps alive illusion and hinders union with the divine. Christianity also believes in one God, but in one whose unity is unique in a complexity that would horrify the Moslem and be misinterpreted altogether by the oriental, whilst it speaks of a personal relationship between God and man that is foreign to both and even to the mysticism which runs through elements at least of all the others. The Christian can hardly recognize in the God of any of the other religions the God he himself knows, while the uncommitted spectator may well reflect that the content of knowledge offered by all the religions together is exceedingly meagre. God remains unknown so long as we remain detached from any particular religion; and how are we to choose which to embrace, if we want to go further?

Hinduism rests upon a long tradition of life and thought, but does not appear to offer any claim to being true that a Western mind can take in. Buddhism offers a way of life rather than a truth, and if we are so obstinate and unfashionable as to ask for truth, it too can offer nothing but the assertion of a teacher who had found the way of enlightenment. Islam offers a book which it claims is a series of infallible, God-dictated propositions. But historical criticism leaves many of these looking more earthly in origin, and shows the dependence of many of the most impressive of them upon the Bible of the Jews or of the Christians. Has Christianity anything more convincing to offer? If so, it can only be the claim that God may truly be known, because he has himself made it possible for us to know him. If such a claim cannot be found true, then God remains the great unknown.

Can metaphysical theism give us the knowledge of God? Metaphysics has flourished on Christian soil, and has been practiced by many of the greatest Christian theologians. Some of these have sought to demonstrate that the existence of God is implied by the existence of a world in which things might be other than they are, while others find in the sense of dependence at the root of personal existence the certainty of the one on whom we depend. In Western Christendom, both Catholic and Protestant, it has until our own day been traditional to begin the exposition of the Christian faith with the proofs of the existence of God. In our own day this procedure is called in question from a variety of angles. Of these the most important for the Christian is the theological criticism which originates from new discoveries in the study of the Bible. Such criticism points out that for the biblical writers God's transcendent holiness means that he may be known only as and when he himself wills, while man's sin means that God can only be known by man as a result of an act which cleanses man from sin at the same time as it discloses God to man's view.

Such criticism of metaphysical or rational theology, and especially of its assertion that there is a knowledge of God independent to some degree of God's self-revelation, has aroused considerable controversy, with which we are not at this stage concerned. Whatever the upshot of the controversy, this at least is clear, that the most that representative theologians of the metaphysical tradition have ever claimed is that theism tells us *that* God *is*, and *what* he *is not*, whereas the truths of the threefold being in unity of God, and of the descent of the Son of God to share our humanity, can be known only by revelation. In other words, the God who really exists, as Christians believe, the God who is the Trinity, who was in his Second Person incarnate as Jesus, cannot be known by theism as such. Moreover, as St Thomas himself makes clear at the beginning of the *Summa Theologica,* such metaphysical ways to the knowledge of God are only for a small minority of men. Nearly all men lack either the mental training or the time for such a philosophical quest. For nearly all men, even God's existence must be known by revelation. For the rest, all theologians are agreed that the theoretical knowledge of God given by theism, whatever its intellectual value, is no substitute for the fully personal knowledge which comes through repentance, faith and obedience. At the most, then, metaphysical theism may give a certain theoretical knowledge of God's existence, and in a negative way, of his attributes; at the least, and this would be the estimate of some of the most weighty of present-day theologians, it gives no knowledge of God worth the name.

Metaphysical theism can also, as we have suggested, be criticized on philosophical grounds. Its basis lies in the intuition of the contingency of the world, that is the realization that the world might not exist or might be otherwise than what it is. From this intuition of contingent being the metaphysician argues to non-contingent, necessary being, that is, to God, whose non-existence is unthinkable, whose nature is self-explanatory, if we could only properly understand him. Everything else requires an explanation, but God is the explanation of everything else, and needs no explanation outside himself.

Some philosophers reply that this is a circular argument. We should not have the idea of contingency unless we had already conceived the by no means obvious idea of necessary being, and so the argument depends upon the hidden assumption of the very thing it purports to prove. On the other hand, even if we do think of the world as contingent, there are existentialist philosophers of our time who can tell us that nothing compels us to draw a theistic conclusion. Man and the world may indeed be poised over the void, but this may simply indicate the absurdity of man's situation—it does not necessarily imply that God has poised him there by giving him this contingent being.

The logical positivists, on the other hand, tell us that there is no way of knowing whether the conclusions of metaphysics are true or not. They do not allege anything whose truth could be verified in any way at all. The world would be just the same if the God of metaphysics did not exist—there are no facts that could be alleged as evidence for his existence that would not also be compatible with his non-existence, and so there can be no meaning in saying that he exists. Believing in him then becomes a matter of taste, over which it is no use arguing. This logical positivist criticism reminds one of the many people today who will tell you that they believe in God, but they do not feel called upon to alter their way of life to conform with this belief. For them, at least, it is clear that a God who 'merely exists' is irrelevant to life, and might as well not be believed in. There is no doubt that a belief in God which stopped short at the theory of theism would be open to this objection, and could not have much in common with what the Christian means by the knowledge of God.

Atheism, like theism, is a metaphysical doctrine. It differs from theism strikingly in asserting God's non-existence: but it does so with the type of method and on the sort of grounds, that theism asserts his existence. As such, it is open to all the same objections as is theism, and seems even harder to prove. But this is not the end of the story for atheism, like theism, seldom flourishes in a passionless soil. Just as theism is in fact rooted in the great historical religions, and in particular in Christianity, so atheism as a metaphysical doctrine is rooted in the rejection of the idea of God as it is proffered by the religions, and in particular by Christianity. Atheism does not seem to flourish very much except in cultures which have been deeply influenced by Christianity.

The real significance of atheism is that it is a rejection either of the God of Christianity as such, or of ideas of him to be found amongst Christians. Atheism is no detached theory, but a passionate rejection of what is felt to be untrue. It therefore merits the respect and attention of Christians in a way that the other alternatives to revelation do not, for it challenges them specifically. While it may well be that at the heart of some forms of atheism is a conscious rejection of the one true and living God who has revealed himself to men in Jesus Christ, a refusal to believe in him because his being is intolerable to the pride of sinful man, it is too easily comforting to be legitimate for Christians to use this explanation as a wholesale condemnation of atheists as exceptional sinners. Such an analysis of atheism, correct as it undoubtedly is in the last resort, is most in place when used by Christians themselves to guide their own self-examination on their own unbelief. We should do better to see in atheism an important criticism of the picture of God which Christians offer to the world as much by their lives as by their doctrines. In that case, it may be proper for Christians to regard atheism as something to be pondered deeply, and used by them gratefully, as a purgation of their own inadequate idea of God. Atheism on this view breaks down the idols which Christians themselves are always apt to set up, and in doing so makes way for the true God who is revealed in Christ.

Any such cursory glance at the alternatives to revelation as the present one must lay itself open to the justifiable criticism that it cannot deal adequately with any of them, that no one who believed passionately in any of the alternatives we have considered would agree for an instant that justice had been done to his convictions. We can have no intention of pretending to consider any of them individually in that sense. Our purpose is a different one. It is to show that revelation is not superfluous, still less that it introduces an element of doubtfulness into a picture that philosophy and comparative religion have made tolerably clear and certain. Our real answer to the alternatives to revelation will become apparent not at this point, but when we expound positively the doctrine of revelation itself.

In the meantime, we may still be justified in concluding that God's existence and nature are not natural certainties for the human mind. An idea of God certainly exists. Underlying the religions of the world is certainly a conviction that there is a higher power than man, with whom man must be in touch if he is to live his life fully. But this idea can be rejected by good and reasonable men without absurdity. The idea of the divine is widespread, but it is rejected most where straight thinking is most valued and practiced, in that part of the world where science has most influenced culture. Moreover, the idea of the divine is vague, and varied in content. Those who accept it mean different and quite incompatible things by it, and outside revelation can offer little reason to support the truth of their ideas. Meanwhile, atheism challenges us to offer men an idea of God that would be truly worthy of him. If man knows of the divine, he does not know what it is, and increasingly he is rejecting religion as something unfitted to the adult stage of human development. If God exists, he is the unknown God, and will remain so unless he makes himself known.

II

The Word of God

CHRISTIANITY comes before the world not as another religion, based on a traditional way of life, or the teaching of some religious genius, nor with a new and more brilliant metaphysics which would not be vulnerable to the criticism of modern philosophy, but as the testimony of men to God's action in history when he revealed himself to the world in Jesus Christ. The Church enters the field not with an argument but with testimony, with the statement (which purports to be the statement of a fact) that the Word has been made flesh and has dwelt among us, that in Jesus of Nazareth, our fellow man, who lived at a certain date in history and from a human point of view takes his place in the history of a certain culture, God has revealed himself finally to all men. For Christianity the truth about God is not an idea but a happening: God has shown himself to us in a historical person. For the Christian Church revelation means above all Jesus Christ; this is so even if we include within its scope what God did in the history of which Jesus Christ is the culmination, and what he has subsequently shown us in the life of the Church of the meaning of supreme revelation in Christ. The Church tells us that God is no longer unknown but known, and known in the person of our fellow man Jesus.

The Christian religion is unique because of Jesus Christ. The part he plays in Christianity is altogether different from the part played by Mohammed in Islam, by the Lord Gautama in Buddhism, or even more by the mythical incarnations in some forms of Hinduism. Mohammed was the recipient of a revelation, Jesus was the giver of a revelation; Gautama was a teacher of what he had discovered. Jesus was sent into the world by God to communicate a truth which is in the last resort identical with himself; the incarnations of Hinduism are myths, and their value in no way depends upon a belief in their historical truth, but Jesus was a living historical person, who existed at a known date, and left a train of historical consequences observable by any unbelieving historian. It is not wrong to say that Christianity *is* Christ, provided that by saying so we do not mean to separate Christ from his Body the Church. All that must be said about the distinctively Christian doctrine of revelation is the consequence of correctly appreciating the centrality of Jesus Christ to Christianity. It is because he is God Incarnate, and the Saviour of the world, that Christianity stands by itself, and is neither religion nor metaphysics, though it may generate both.

In the first place, then, Christianity is not one of the religions, because it is the revelation of God in Christ. It is characteristic of religion to explain the world from the world, that is to help men to bear the pressures of life, suffering, the problem of evil, crises in personal life, by means of myths drawn from human experience of the world, though they usually purport to refer to 'another world' on which this depends. A typical example is the fertility myth of death and rebirth, made famous by the *Golden Bough*; this provides both a myth and a magically efficacious ritual whereby the insecurity of man in a changing world can be understood hopefully and his needs met by the propitiation of the deity. The Greek myths are the imaginative personifications of the natural forces with which man is confronted in his own mind and in the world in which he lives, and it is surely this that accounts for their abiding symbolic power in the human mind. They correspond to the world which man knows and to his inner experience. The oriental religions take man's experience of the meaninglessness of life without ethical or social purpose, and teach him that behind the illusion of change and multiplicity is an underlying unity in which peace is to be found. In the same way, they build on man's experience of poverty in an undeveloped country, and teach men to do without on the bodily level for the sake of the soul. This kind of religion, whether clothed in myth as in some forms of Hinduism, or presented as metaphysical mysticism as

27

in other forms of Hinduism or in Buddhism, offers man an escape by way of abstraction from life. But the abstract, immanent God of oriental religion is in the last resort an abstraction from *the world*. He is that which underlies all that is in the world, and is indeed its inmost reality. Islam is in a special case because it is so dependent upon the Bible, but here again, though the transcendent God of the Prophet is himself conceived in terms learned from the Old Testament, his predestinating will is thought of partly on the model of the inexorability of natural law and the harshness of desert life. Nor is he truly revealed. After he has given the Koran to Mohammed he remains as unknown as before. All that is known is certain statements about him. Neither the oriental immanent God nor the Islamic transcendent deity is a living Lord who is personally revealed.

It is therefore characteristic of the religions that they are non-historical, that they are based upon permanent features and characteristics of the world. Christianity, on the contrary, is based upon a revelation given at a particular time and place. Thus Christianity is not primarily a cosmology, that is an explanation of the world, which starts from the world and seeks to account for its existence and character, but a theology, a 'word about God', which starts from him who makes himself known as other than the world by acting personally within the sphere of man's life. By doing particular things, by making a difference in the world through events which might not otherwise have happened, God draws man's attention to himself as a reality which could not have been inferred from the permanent elements in the world. God conveys his uniqueness to man by revealing himself historically, and not by inserting the idea of himself into the mental furniture of all men at all times.

This 'particularity' of the Christian revelation has always been a stumbling block to the human mind, for philosophically speaking it implies what might be called the contingency of the Absolute, in a way which oriental religion in all its forms does not. It seems to deny God's infinity in favour of his concreteness, and so to make God in the image of the creation—

precisely what a moment ago we have accused the religions of doing. It will become apparent as we proceed how wide of the mark this charge in fact is, but it will inevitably be made, for God is indeed more concerned with his own concreteness as the person who confronts us and asks for our personal allegiance, than he is with asserting his philosophical attributes. The God revealed in Christ is no abstraction, but one who evokes decision, worship or rejection. He is not the 'something behind everything somewhere' but a living person, who is other than the world he has made, and must be known as a person.

Thirdly, it is characteristic of the religions to leave the world as it is, but of Christianity to seek to change the world in accordance with God's will. No doubt this is not the most fundamental element in Christianity, for nothing can be as important for the Christian as to adore God simply because he is what he is, but this adoration will always lead to action of some kind, by way of intercession (action in prayer) or by obedience in the world. Christians who deplore modern science and technology misconceive their own faith, and would gain a clearer insight into its nature from their brethren who live in Moslem or Hindu countries. I remember on a visit to Algiers being struck, as others have been, by the difference between the Kasbah, where the Islamic people of the country live, and the European quarter. In the one, squalor, filth and disease were evident everywhere, as they had always been; in the other, sanitation, cleanliness and the comforts and conveniences of a modern European city presented an unforgettable contrast to the neighbouring Arab city.

The difference between the two quarters of Algiers is theological. The Kasbah is inhabited by men who have been taught resignation, because God wills all things to be as they are. The European quarter was built by men who have learned from the Christian tradition that the Son of God came into the world to struggle with evil in all its forms and to defeat it, and that men are called to share in his victory and to spread it. This is one more consequence of the historical and particular nature of Christianity. The world as it stands does not give an adequate

29

clue to God's will. His moral purposes are revealed by his own acts in history. He is to be served in history, in the real world, and not by an escape from it into a peace which is won only by being detached from one's neighbour and his needs.

Christianity is not a religion, in the sense that the great religions of the world are so called. Nevertheless, Christianity from the point of view of one who does not believe in it will necessarily be classed with the religions; Christians themselves, by a loose way of talking, frequently, in this country at least, refer to Christianity as 'religion'. It might therefore nevertheless be convenient to follow the example of many British theologians and call Christianity *revealed* religion. In the same way, Christianity will appear to the unbeliever, for example to a logical positivist philosopher, as a form of metaphysics (though it is not in fact metaphysical), because it speaks about God, and makes statements about realities which cannot be discovered by the techniques of science. It is on this account that many theologians feel called upon to vindicate the possibility of metaphysical speech in general, when they enter into controversy with the positivist philosophers. There may be some philosophical value in this enterprise, but it has no advantages from the point of view of Christian theology, because Christianity is not metaphysical (if at all) in the same sense as metaphysical theism. Christians know God through Jesus Christ, rather than through metaphysical arguments about the cause or ground of the being of man or the world. Metaphysics offers a line of argument which starts from the world as we know it by common sense, science, or the philosophical criticism of experience, whether of the world or of the self, and ends in the God who is held to be implied by the data from which the metaphysician has started.

The important point is that the metaphysician, starting from data which are in principle accessible to everybody, from features of the world which are always the case, in all places and at all times, and using arguments whose formal validity ought to be acceptable to all competent judges, seeks to establish something new and not previously conceded, the being of

God. From the point of view of persons whose upbringing is scientific, the drawback of this apparently advantageous enterprise is that the metaphysician appears to be presenting a hypothesis, which ought to be capable of being proved or disproved. His hypothesis or theory ought to depend on evidence which could be checked experimentally against a control. But the metaphysician's evidence is not of this kind. He cannot suggest any experiment which might prove or disprove his theory, for in principle his theory is an attempt to harmonize all the evidence there is, to account for the whole world. He is generalizing to the last degree.

The Christian Church, on the other hand, starts from certain concrete facts, in particular the life, death and resurrection of Jesus Christ, and asserts that in them God is revealed. If God is known in particular events, there is even a sense in which Christianity is theoretically disprovable.[1] If a more skilful historical technique could prove that the life and death of Jesus was a literary fiction, as a few persons have occasionally supposed (as indeed seems to be the official Marxist line), then Christianity could not be true. Again, it might be suggested that the verification of Christianity lies in the fact that when in repentance and faith we commit ourselves to Jesus Christ, we are actually brought into personal touch with God.

In the same way, just because Christianity is based on God's revelation of himself in Christ, it cannot be experienced from the standpoint of the detached observer but only from that of the committed disciple. The philosopher may believe and know that this is the Son of God, but if so he will do so upon the apostolic testimony to Jesus Christ, and not as a philosopher. It follows that Christianity cannot be proved in advance of commitment, like a theorem in mathematics, where everything is already given. It is based upon fact, not theory. It is characteristic of facts that they cannot be proved or disproved *a priori*, by a theory which asserts that something must have happened for reasons of appropriateness, or could not

[1] For a fuller discussion of the rationality of Christian faith, see below, Chapter V.

have happened because this is not compatible with what we think the nature of the world is. You have to go and look, to see if the facts are there or not. If they are there, you have to amend your theory to fit. The scientist only recognizes as facts what he can verify by observation or repeat in a controlled experiment. He then regards them as evidence for a law.

The Christian faith is based on facts of a different kind, which are in the nature of the case unrepeatable and not subject to experiment. Nor do they point to a law, but to that which is precisely unique. The only kind of proof, if that is the right word, which can be offered for facts of this kind is not scientific and experimental but historical, that is, the evidence of eyewitnesses, and this is the kind of evidence which the foundation documents of Christianity do in fact offer. We have to ask whether the eyewitnesses are consistent and credible, and whether their evidence has been correctly transmitted, and not whether they speak of the kind of thing that happens. Of course, resurrections and virgin births don't happen. There can be no scientific law about them. But perhaps the Virgin Birth and the Resurrection did happen in the one and only crucial case. If so, there will be the evidence of those who were involved in the events, and we must make up our minds whether to accept it or not. It may seem peculiar and offensive that God has linked the knowledge of himself to such unrepeatable and therefore unscientific happenings, but that according to Christianity is what he has done. The advantages will become more apparent the more fully we grasp the revelation which was thus made.

There is another and subtler reason to distinguish Christianity from metaphysics, and to assert its historical nature. God has revealed himself by an act which at the same time restores the broken relationship of the world to himself, and the broken relationship of the parts of the world to one another. There cannot be a harmonious metaphysical system embracing God and the world and all the parts of the world in a harmonious whole, because of the presence of evil in the world. Evil, the 'flaw in the universe', means that no account of the world as a whole can be given, except from the standpoint of faith, of those who know that the world is held together and bound to God by Christ on the Cross, and not otherwise. Revelation accordingly is an action taken by God, which reveals him to a world which did not know him, and reveals the world to itself as his world, in the teeth of the evidence. We cannot by metaphysics construct a harmonious doctrine of God and creation, and then add to it as a second stage the special Christian doctrines of the redemption of the world and of the Incarnation, and so of God as Trinity. We must rather approach the creation through the Incarnation and the Resurrection, as a later chapter will endeavour to make clear. The historical character of Christianity is linked to the fact that it is the work of God in redeeming a fallen world, and from that act of redemption the Christian revelation cannot be separated.

It has so far been maintained that the aspect of the Christian revelation which distinguishes it most sharply from all other possible ways to God is that God has made himself known on his own initiative, through the historical person of Jesus Christ, in the act of reconciling a fallen world to himself. We have now to see how Jesus Christ reveals God. Jesus according to the testimony of St John is the Word made flesh. The first and most obvious meaning of this statement is that he is the revelation of God in human form. The Word of God in the Old Testament (the best clue to the meaning of the New) is God's speech to man, uttered through his prophets, telling his people of his character, will and intentions. Because it is God's Word, it is no mere word, but act as well. When God speaks, something happens, for what he says, goes. His Word does not return to him void, empty, but it accomplishes that for which he sent it forth. Just as in human affairs, at some crisis, a word spoken may be in the fullest sense an event, something which happens and so transforms a situation as much as any action could, the Word which God utters is always full of significance, is always an action as much as a word. So the men of the Old Testament, as they reflected on their experience of the power of God's word, came to see that he had created the world by his Word. 'By the word of God were the heavens made', for when God said, 'Let there be a firmament', there was a firmament. The creation story in Genesis, with all its profound doctrine of the creative Word, was written by men who belonged to a people which had already known the prophetic word and its power, who had been sent in exile by the word of judgement uttered through the prophets.

The men of the New Testament applied the term 'word' to the Gospel which the Church proclaimed, to the story of the birth, teaching, death and resurrection of Jesus, of his exaltation to the right hand of God, his sending of the Spirit and his future coming to judge the world, and the call to decision with which the proclamation inevitably ended. Like the prophets they experienced the power and activity of God's Word, when they saw that it was never without result—when it was preached, some believed, but others became hostile and stirred up persecution. The Gospel when it was preached divided men into two groups, in a manner that clearly prefigured, though it did not foreclose, the final judgement. Judgement and mercy were equally latent in this story that was told, and by hearing it men met with God and so either experienced his forgiveness or were hardened in their rebellion.

Jesus Christ was the content of the story, and so it was a natural development when St John applied to him the title of the Word of God, and believing as he did in his pre-existence as the Son whom the Father had sent into the world, saw that he always had been the Word of God, that God had created all things by him, that he had always been making himself known through the one who in the fullness of time had been made flesh, and dwelt among us. 'In the beginning was the Word, and the Word was with God, and the Word was God.' But to call Jesus the Word was not only to explain Jesus, it was also greatly to deepen the meaning of the revealing word. It meant that revelation was personal, that when God speaks of himself he speaks not in sentences and phrases, but in one who is a person, as he is. Jesus Christ is the Word of God because he is the Son of God; he brings grace and truth because he has the glory as

34

of the only-begotten of the Father. He is God of God, Light of Light, 'consubstantial'[1] with the Father, and so he that has seen him has seen the Father, for he and the Father are one. Jesus Christ can reveal God not only because he knows him at first hand, because he *knows* what God is, but also because he *is* what God is. He does not merely bring information about God, he brings God himself.

Thus the Christian doctrine of revelation is inseparable from the Christian faith in the Incarnation of the Word, and from the doctrine of the Trinity. If God makes himself truly known in Jesus Christ, then Jesus is God as well as man, and in God's own unity of being there are mysterious differentiations and relationships, which we can best conceive of by putting together the models of a man and his word, and of a man and his son. God the Father eternally utters himself in a word that perfectly reflects all that he himself is; God the Son perfectly mirrors the being of his Father, and the two are one, for there are not two Gods but one God in two ways of being. The Father and the Son have not a similar but the same being, and yet this being exists in two ways, at each end of a fully personal relationship of love. The Sonship of the Word is the foundation of the Incarnation, for man too is called to be the son of God, and he who as God is eternally the perfect Son becomes man in time to live out man's perfect sonship also. Man too is created in the image of God, and so the divine Son images God in human form as he lives out sonship unaffected and undamaged by sin. In Christ the Son we see perfect God and perfect man; his human sonship echoes with equal perfection on its own level his divine sonship. He lives out the life of God on the human scale and so he shows us both what God is and what we are, and continually refuse to be.

Thus as we meditate upon Jesus Christ we are led, as the Apostles themselves were, from the perfect and sinless humanity of Jesus, who is all that man was meant to be, who gives full meaning for the first time to the Old Testament story of Adam, because he is the Son of Man and the New

[1] Gk. *homoousios*. cf. the Nicene Creed: 'being of one substance with the Father'.

Adam, who is the Image of God and so, like the Messianic King of Psalm 2, the Son of God, up the scale of revelation to his divinity and oneness with the Father as the divine Son and Word, and so finally to the Father himself, who is what the Son is, for the Son is one with him. Thus it is that Jesus our fellow man is the revelation of God as well as of perfect manhood, for he reflects God flawlessly on the human scale, in perfectly fulfilling the original calling of man. And so we human beings, who could never understand God in the majesty and holiness of his being in heaven, can understand him in our way and in a manner fitted to the limitations of the human mind, and yet without error, for the scaling down is perfect in every detail, because Jesus Christ is the Image of God. God is like Jesus: such is the testimony of the Christian revelation to the nature of God.

How then does Jesus convey to us the first-hand knowledge of God which he himself possesses by nature? Primarily by living out in our midst a perfect human life, making of human birth, growth, speech, action, suffering and death the mirror of the holy love of God. We cannot isolate Jesus' revelation of God in what he said about God, for so often what he said was simply the interpretation of his actions. Christmas and Easter show us God even more clearly than the Sermon on the Mount, for there we know for certain and without possibility of misunderstanding that God is love. Jesus acts out the nature of God upon the human scene, and appeals to our insight to recognize the picture. Thus everything that Jesus is, says and does is revelatory of God; in that life nothing is insignificant, for nothing is wasted or imperfect, everything is done in perfect fulfilment of the will of God. His life has its high-points, as the commemorations of the Church's year make clear, and it culminates in the saving Passion. But nothing is irrelevant or without meaning: God is in everything.

For the first disciples, everything was simple, if they could only believe. To know Jesus was to know God. They were friends with their Creator, and like Adam and Eve in the garden walked and talked with God. And yet nothing can be plainer from their own accounts of the matter than their inability really to believe. Nothing in the tradition of their people had prepared them for Incarnation; confused notions of a Messiah were of little help when they were confronted with the reality. They never really assimilated the truth that the Son of Man must suffer. At Caesarea Philippi they confessed him for the Son of God, meaning by that perhaps no more than that he was the Messianic King of prophecy. But it was what was required of them. They were ready to be taught the secret of the Suffering Servant of God, and to see in Jesus transfigured the glory of man in the image of God, shining with the uncreated light. But the cloud obscured the visible glory, and they were left to follow along the hard road to Jerusalem and Calvary, and to witness the true glory in the bitterness of death. But only after the resurrection could they see the glory for what it was, and pierce through the shame to read its divine meaning. Indeed, Jesus did not fully become the revelation of God for them until he had been exalted to the right hand of God and had sent them the Spirit by which they knew him as Lord. In the end, they do not appear to have enjoyed advantages over subsequent generations of believers. At the time when humanly speaking they were closest to Jesus, the Cross and the Resurrection with the Ascension had not yet given them the key to his life; subsequently, when the indwelling Spirit made them closer to Jesus than they had been when he was on earth, they were in the same position as their descendants in the Church—they knew God through Christ, but by faith and in the Holy Spirit. We who believe on the basis of their testimony know God as fully as they.

Thus, though the revelation of God is given at one point in time, in the life and death and resurrection of Jesus, it can be received at any time from then until the end of history. The Word was made flesh in order that he might be proclaimed 'to the ends of the earth and to the end of the world'.[1] The first disciples found Jesus to be the revelation of the inmost heart of God as the Holy Spirit lighted up their personal memories of

[1] Newbigin, *The Household of God*, p. 132.

him. We find him so when we believe in him in the power of the same Holy Spirit, but on the testimony to Jesus of the first disciples, recorded in Scripture and passed on by the living Church. Thus the revelation, given once and for all at one point in space and time, is to be proclaimed to all men and through the rest of time, that the world may believe that God has sent Jesus into the world, and that he is the truth. Jerusalem at the beginning of the first century is the starting point of the world mission of the Church, whose object is the proclamation of the Word to all men everywhere and until the end of time. With the preaching of the Word goes the power of the Spirit, clearing away the veil from men's minds that they may see God in the face of Jesus Christ, and repenting of their sins, be baptized into the Church, which is the Body of Christ, continuing his saving mission until his return.

Thus it is now through the Church that we come to find Jesus, the revelation of God. Before he ascended into heaven, he gave his Church the commission that he had received from the Father. 'As the Father hath sent me, even so I send you.' 'Go ye into all the world and preach the Gospel.' The Word and the Spirit continue the revelatory work through the mission of the Catholic Church. Not that anything new can be revealed, for nothing can be added to perfection. But new men must hear and believe, and the Church must grow in the understanding of what is given once and for all. The work of revelation goes on as men find Christ in the message and life of the Church, and find him the same yesterday and today and for ever, the open way to God.

Christ ascended into heaven when he had finished his work on earth, and sat down at the right hand of the Father. But the finished work must be proclaimed, and men initiated into his endless life. And so, though from one point of view Christ's work of revelation, as of reconciliation, is completed, he is still at work in his Body the Church applying that completed work to the rest of humanity. Wherever he sends his Church, he goes invisibly too, to be known through the Holy Spirit in the preaching of the Church, in the Bible, and in the sacramental life of the Church. The Spirit reveals Christ's continual presence in the Church which is his Body, and so in the Church today, as in the historic life of Jesus, God stands revealed through Christ.

The historicity and uniqueness of Christ apply equally to his Body. If there is no sure way to God outside Christ, there is no sure way to God outside the Church. The Church is the place where the revelation lives on, and outside her faith and life the old darkness lingers. The Church, which is the Body of Christ and the community of the Holy Spirit, is the link between the earthly life of Christ and the men of every age. In her God has provided a living bond with the Christ of Nazareth and Calvary, so that we know him not merely as past but as present, and so know God in living reality. The authority of the Church has nothing to do with the superior insights of her members, whether laity or Pope, but with the continual living presence of Christ her Head, ever active through the Word and Sacraments, and in the life of the community, to reveal God to the world. The Church is nothing in herself, but she is the Body of Christ, and the instrument therefore of his unceasing work of revelation, as his personal body was before his Passion. It is the glory and privilege of the members of the Church, who are themselves sinners, that they can be, through the action of their Head in his members, the means of bringing others to the knowledge and love of God.

III

God Reveals Himself

THE God who reveals himself in Jesus Christ reveals himself as a person, but in his revelation of himself he does not cease to be the mysterious God. He reveals himself to us of his own will, for without his self-revelation we should not know him. He reveals himself, and not in the first instance truths about himself which might be possessed outside a personal relationship to him. For he reveals himself as a person, and not as an abstraction, a living Lord and not some Absolute or First Cause, as one who knows and loves men, and wills to be known and loved by them. And finally, he reveals himself while remaining the supreme mystery: indeed it is precisely as mystery that he reveals himself, for he is the Holy One, though the Holy One who loves the world.

God *reveals* himself. It is part of the meaning of the fact that God is God that he is to be known at his will and not ours. The Bible is full of the thought of God as holy. This means that there is between God and man what Kierkegaard has called 'the infinite qualitative distinction'. God differs from ourselves not merely in degree, as would be the case if we were both spirits, and he the greatest of spirits, but in kind. He is above us not only morally but ontologically, as he is above everything else that he has made, far removed from us in the majesty of his divine being. He is above everything that we can conceive, and any image that we could form of him, even the highest mental image, would be a travesty of what he really is, an insult to the divine majesty. Such is the meaning of the second Commandment, and such is the unvarying testimony of the Bible and of Christian experience.

He is not present as an object to our thought. The highest conception that we can form in our minds is not yet God, by far. He is beyond the horizon of our minds, and if all depended on us he would be for ever unknown. The creature cannot know the Creator, as he knows us; the relationship is one way only. In saying this we are not in the least expressing pessimism about man's reason in its own sphere. There is nothing in the world that man's reason may not find out and know, no spiritual or aesthetic value that is beyond the grasp of man. But God is holy, and a god who could be known by the human mind would *ipso facto* be betrayed as not the God of whom the biblical revelation speaks, but one of the spiritual values, a part of what we call the world, of the sphere over which man by divine appointment has dominion, and so an idol, a worldly object set up as a false divinity. Such is the implication of the biblical teaching about God.

But the Bible also teaches something that seems paradoxically opposed to this, for it tells us that God wills to be known by man, and indeed requires of man the knowledge of God. God, who made man because he loved him, does not grudge man the knowledge of himself. God wills to make of man his friend, his child, his son, and holds out to him the hope of knowing God even as God now knows man. This is in fact the very destiny to which man is called, and against the truth that intrinsically man cannot know the Holy God must be placed the complementary truth that man was made for the knowledge of God, that the Vision of God is to be man's beatitude. If we try to do away with the paradox that the unknowable God wills to be known, modifying the statement that God is instrinsically unknowable in order to assert that man can at the peak of some mystical ascent at last climb up to the knowledge of God, we make the knowledge of God natural, so that it ceases to be the loving gift of God. The knowledge of God is always given to us by an act of grace. Man cannot as it were claim it as a right inherent in being human.

From another point of view, however, it is indeed part of the calling of humanity to know God. Man who has not the knowledge of God is unnatural, and cannot take his natural place at the head of the creation, to rule it in God's name as

God created him to do. Dependence upon God's grace is natural to man, although he can carry on his existence without it, and so great are the powers of man's mind even without God's grace that he may not realize the lack of the crowning knowledge of his Creator. Jesus Christ, the only perfectly natural man, knew God in dependence upon his gracious gift of knowledge, and never for an instant repudiated his dependence, but rather constantly affirmed it as the pre-condition of his true knowledge.[1]

In the Old Testament myth of the creation, man is represented as knowing God while he keeps to his commandments. Man and God live together in the Paradisal state in unclouded intercourse. God walks and talks with Adam in the Garden in the cool of the day. But the Fall interrupts this relationship. Man shuts out God by disobeying him, and is given over to idolatry by God. Man preserves a kind of racial memory of the God he does not know, and makes gods of his own to replace him. But since man now knows only the world, and, because he is a sinner, fundamentally does not wish to know God, he makes his gods from the worldly things that he knows. Man's gods are not now far above him, but on his own level or below it. He may fear them, projecting the guilt of his sinful heart upon the gods he worships, and attributing to them barbarous and cruel desires, or he may admire them as one admires a landscape or a sunset or a work of art, but in neither case does he have a Lord, to whom he owes unconditional allegiance. He does not 'know the Lord.'

Though the breach with God breaks up man's personal life, since he who is not at peace with God cannot be at peace with his neighbour, man's rational powers remain unimpaired in so far as they are directed on the world. He is capable of culture and civilization, of economic and technological advance, but he cannot solve the problem of God. For God can only be known by his own gift, and man cannot receive this gift except by being redeemed by God from his sin, and put back into true relationship with the Creator. And so God must make a

[1] v. John 5. 19f., 30; 7. 28f.; 8. 28, 40, 54f., etc.

second creation. A second Adam must come upon the scene of history, who will willingly know God by grace. Christ is the head of a second human race, as well as the Son of God. Divinely and humanly, he knows God as God wills to be known, and mediates this knowledge to those who are to be the members of the second humanity.

God's revelation in Christ, the basis of the New Creation, shows us what the first was meant to be. The New Adam is not a myth, like the first, but a historical person, through whom alone we can truly understand the prophetic myth. In the revelation in Christ we see clearly and unmistakably that the knowledge of God is the gift of God, that it can come to us only if God reveals himself by coming down from heaven and showing himself to us, and if he cleanses our hearts from sin as we repent and turn back to him. The healings of the blind and the deaf by Christ show symbolically how man's being has to be opened up again to God by grace, before man can receive the knowledge that God wills to give him, without which man cannot please God.

Both by creation and by redemption, therefore, man depends upon grace for the knowledge of God. God is not open to our inspection, but as the Holy One, who is high and lifted up above all things that are made, he must will to be known if he is to be known at all. It follows that we must recognize that the knowledge of God by revelation is grounded in a divine decision that man shall know him, taken by God out of love for man. God takes that decision in the sovereign freedom and ungrudging love that are his very nature. He wills to be with us, in order that we may be with him. Revelation is an act of God, in his supra-temporal being, which is expressed at man's level in acts in history. God shows that revelation is an act of his love precisely in not diffusing the knowledge of himself over the whole human race, so that man might mistake it for an achievement of his own, but by linking it to the historical happening of the coming of Jesus, the Messiah of Israel. A doctrine of the knowledge of God which made it out to be a human achievement would be as dangerous to the true life of the Church as a similar doctrine in the realm of the love of God. There is a 'Pelagianism' in the realm of knowledge which is as false to the foundation of the Church as the original heresy of that name which made man's good works the fruit of his own efforts, even if aided by God. Our dependence upon revelation for the knowledge of God is total, not partial, although we were created for that very knowledge.

Revelation means, then, that God of his own free will and because he loves us has drawn aside the veil that hides him from us, and has shown himself to us as he is. Just as we must not in the slightest degree minimize the truth that revelation is God's act and not man's achievement, so we must not in any degree minimize the completeness of the act of revelation when it comes, for both errors minimize the love of God for men. God reveals *himself*. He does not, like the God of Islam, hide himself behind a series of infallible propositions in a book, nor behind some doctrinal system. There is not, beyond the revelation in Christ, some further, still hidden area of God's being which might conceivably be quite different from those aspects of him which we knew in Christ. Nor is there some conceivable other and further revelation of him, which might be given later in human history, or to some other planet. God is without qualification what he shows himself to be in Christ. His being cannot be split up into parts: if he is revealed at all he is revealed totally. This is what we mean by denying the Arian heresy, and asserting our faith that Christ is God of God, Light of Light, very God of very God, of one substance with the Father. In Christ we find nothing less than God. He that hath seen him hath seen the Father.

God has revealed himself, then, by coming into this world in person and dwelling among us, so that we could see his glory. Jesus Christ is not a messenger from God, entrusted with a description of the one who sent him, but God incarnate —his message is himself. This is so simple that it is exceptionally difficult to grasp. We always want to think of revelation as the communication of truths. We identify it with a corpus of infallible doctrine, or with a Bible that is verbally inspired.

The simplicity of the revelation itself eludes the grasp of our minds. Revelation is simply the person who was in our midst, who lives on in heaven and in his Body on earth. God loves us more than we suppose, reveals himself more fully than we dare to believe, and yet by that very fact refuses to show himself to us in such a way that we can ever finally codify his revelation in a series of statements.

An inspired Bible is necessary, and we have it. True doctrine is necessary also, and this too we have in the formulated dogmas of the Church. But both of these are true because they point truly to Jesus Christ, who is himself God revealed. They are revelation at one remove, Jesus Christ is revelation itself. We can never fully say what he has revealed, we can only look at Christ and see God. In the ineffable unity of his divine and human person there is always more than we can say in words, even though the words may be a true description of him, so far as they go. Indeed, it is of the greatest importance that the Church should describe Christ correctly, when she sets out to do so, and she has the guidance of the Holy Spirit in discharging that responsibility. It is certainly possible to describe Christ otherwise than as he is, and so to falsify the revelation. But if we fall into the error of identifying Bible or Church doctrine with the revelation, we are minimizing the love of God, for he has given us nothing less than himself. It is in reflection upon revelation that we construct our doctrines, we are receiving revelation when we contemplate Christ and see him as our Lord and our God.

It follows that we cannot distinguish in God's revelation of himself between his existence and his attributes, or between metaphysical and ethical aspects of his being. God shows himself to us as a whole, existence, attributes and character all at once. Jesus is in every sense the evidence for God. He comes to us with first-hand knowledge, and tells us of God as he really is. We must believe him on his own authority, because he convinces us that he speaks from personal knowledge, and because his life and his teaching reinforce the impression of his perfect integrity. Certainly, man did not hear of God for the first time when Jesus came to us. We shall see in the next chapter how the revelation in Christ was prepared for by previous acts of God in history. But nowhere in the Bible, and certainly not in the life or teaching of Christ, do we find any suggestion that the existence of God can ever be argued about. Christ would surely not have answered a doubter by an argument, but would have spoken of the Father from his own direct knowledge of him. The right way to convince a person of the reality of God is not to argue about his existence but to speak of him as he is, as through Christ we know him to be. There is no such being as a God who merely exists: he would rightly be found far more incredible than the God and Father of our Lord Jesus Christ, who is holy love, who has revealed himself and saved the world by his acts in history. You cannot divide the simplicity of God's being into his existence and his nature, or into his unity as the creator and his triplicity as redeemer, for to speak of only a part of God is to speak of a God who does not exist. God is shown to us in his revelation in the unity and simplicity of his personal life, and if we do not see him there we shall see him nowhere.

If, however, we turn away from the direct contemplation of God in Christ, from the act of receiving revelation, which is fundamentally an act of faith and of prayer, in order to think about him, as we also must, in order that our contemplation of him may be a rich and full act of understanding and not a gazing into vacancy, then we shall find ourselves analysing, if the word may be permitted, the God who there shows himself to us. The God who is revealed in Christ has many aspects, but his character can be fruitfully explored if we begin to think of him under the two somewhat contrasted aspects of holiness and love, which meet in the unity of his personal life. Holiness refers to his infinite exaltation over all that he has made, whereby we know him as the Lord.

Under his holiness we can range the metaphysical attributes of omnipotence, omniscience, incomprehensibility or omnipresence, and aseity, which may legitimately arise in the mind as we reflect upon the fact he is revealed as creator, as well as the moral attributes of supreme purity and hatred of all evil. Under his love we think of his grace in creating and redeeming the world and in destining man for beatitude in union with his own life, as well as his willingness to reveal himself to us, and to reconcile us to himself by the forgiveness of our sins. Thus in terms of the present discussion, God's holiness means that he must *reveal* himself if he is to be known, and his love means that he does reveal and that he reveals *himself*. To trace in detail how our picture of God is related to the acts of Christ would be the subject matter for another study, as well as of the constant meditation of every Christian. But in Christ, with his dignity and humility, his freedom and his service of all men, his inexorable demand for perfection, and his bringing of forgiveness to the publicans and sinners, his call to the cross and his self-giving in his own Cross, we see God's holy love acted out in its mysterious unity. Every action of Christ shows us what God is, and every facet is but a facet of a unity that transcends description and could indeed only be lived out.

In particular, God reveals himself to us as a person. Outside the revelation in Christ, men often ask if God is personal, and as often as not come to the conclusion that he is not. Indeed, if we go to the idea of God by way of metaphysics, there is no necessary reason to think of God as personal. Why should pure being be personal? Why should one who is known chiefly as the cause of the world have any interest in personal relationships with mere men? If we knew nothing of God in Christ, we should find it hard to answer. The God of metaphysics cannot be other than an abstraction, for the holiness of God bars any concrete knowledge of him by that route. The Absolute may disdain to know the relative, the Unmoved Mover may, as Aristotle thought, not even know that he moves. Christians may find these questions unreal, for they cannot think metaphysically without calling in what they know by revelation, and the terms of Aristotle can hardly be read without the overtones of the biblical theology of St Thomas or the poetry and devotion of Dante. But a metaphysics that leans not at all on the Christian revelation may well posit an impersonal God, or a

God whose personality is utterly remote from what we mean by the word.

But the God and Father of our Lord Jesus Christ is a person. Christ shows us divine and human personality, and gives us the measure of the meaning of the word. Indeed it has been suggested that as a matter of history the idea of human personality is a fruit of the reflection of Christians upon the revelation of God in Christ. It was as theologians meditated upon the meaning of personality in God that they came to understand it in man. We are persons above all in relationship. God shows himself to be a person by entering into relationship with men, though Christians have come to see that he already experiences personal relationship within his own threefold being before there is any question of the creation of man. God reveals himself as knowing and loving men, and desiring them to know and love him. And so he makes each of us a person, when he addresses us in his Word and in Holy Baptism, calling us by our name, and making us responsible for our lives to him. Divine personality makes human personality through revelation. The God who loves us is a person.

It is thus consonant with all that we have so far seen of God and his revelation that he should show himself to be a person by revealing himself in a person. Indeed, it is just because God reveals himself in Jesus Christ that we are entitled to speak of him as a person. The Word of God, as we have seen, is personal, not a message but a man. He addresses himself therefore not to our minds only, but to our whole capacity for personal response to another person, ultimately therefore to our love. In giving us his love in Christ incarnate and crucified he creates in us true personality by lifting us up to personal intercourse with himself. In clinging to Jesus Christ as the true revelation of God we find the certainty that God is a person who cares for us. And so, as we shall see, the only proper human analogy for the knowledge of God is the knowledge we have of other persons.

No doubt in saying this we should have to guard ourselves against the assumption that personality as we know it provided a key to the being of God. To think that would be to fall into precisely the non-revelational approach to theology which will lead us astray when we think of the holy God. Such is the error of theologians who assume that God had to create the world, in order to have some object for his love, in order to have an answering subject with whom he might be in relationship. Such a view detracts from the holiness of God the creator, and with it his love which it purports to assert, for only the love of the Holy One, who does not need the world he makes, can be truly gracious. In such a view God becomes correlative to the world, and so either God is limited or the world deified. In either case we are far from Christian ground. It seems that such a danger lurks behind the present tendency to personalism in theology, associated with the I-Thou philosophy of Martin Buber, from which many, including the present writer, have learned much.

If God is revealed to us in Christ as a person, then we do well to remember that he is still the holy person, and that personality in him must mean something far profounder than anything we know in human experience. We cannot make deductions about the life of God from what we know of personal relationships in fallen humanity. And in fact, we find that a fuller reflection on the revelation in Christ has shown the Church that God is not just a person, but three persons in one God—though there is an ambiguity in that statement, arising from the fact that 'person' meant for the Fathers who formulated the doctrine of the Trinity something different from and less rich than the modern conception of personality. Since it is not our purpose here to expound the content of the Christian revelation, let us content ourselves with saying that God is not a person as we are persons, but more so. In the complexity of relationships within the Trinity we find a personal life that transcends anything that we know of personality for ourselves. Nevertheless, it is fundamental to our understanding of God that he reveals himself in a person and therefore as a person.

The cautions of the last paragraph bring us to the last of the themes of this chapter. We are warned against the intrusions of conceptions of God derived from other sources than the revelation by the reflection that God does not cease to be holy in lovingly revealing himself. On the contrary, he is holy precisely in the self-revelation which he makes in Christ. That is to say, his revelation of himself does not remove the mystery of his being, but rather discloses that it *is* mystery. While we cannot exaggerate the fullness and completeness of God's self-revelation, the mode of that revelation is in Jesus Christ, the suffering Servant of God. God does not come to us in the unveiled majesty of his glory, for no man could see that and live. Revelation has a certain indirectness, which distinguishes it from the Day of Judgement. On that final day, God will be shown to us in the undimmed brightness of his glory, and in that blinding light all things and all men will be shown for what they really are and always have been. Our God is a consuming fire, in which all that does not partake of the righteousness Christ brought will be burnt up. It is of God's loving mercy to man that he reveals himself in a mystery that leaves us the possibility of making a decision for him. We are inconceivably foolish if we wish the knowledge of God to be perfectly clear, and all difficulties removed. For then we should stand condemned for our failure to know and love God. Even the revelation in Christ brings a judgement with it, for though Christ did not come into the world to condemn the world, but that the world might be saved through him, there is a condemnation which inevitably falls on those who love darkness rather than light, because their deeds are evil.[1]

And so God hides his divine majesty from us in the humility of the Suffering Servant, and is revealed supremely in the Cross. In the mystery of the Cross, to the Jews a stumbling block and to the Greeks foolishness, the power and wisdom and glory of God's kingdom are fully revealed. The glory that played about Christ as he taught and healed in Galilee seems all dimmed as he comes to the Cross, to die as an unknown criminal a death that filled all men with horror. Only in irony is his true identity hinted at in the superscription above the Cross: '*Jesus*

[1] John 3.19.

Nazarenus, Rex Juadaeorum'. And yet the mystery of the Passion reveals as nothing else does the love and glory of God. Only the Cross tells us for certain that God is love, but it tells us so in a manner which leaves no doubt that we are there confronted with the supreme mystery.

Mystery has surrounded the identity of Christ from the beginning of his public life. According to St Mark, Jesus deliberately kept his Messiahship secret until he was in a position to correct, by his own teaching to his disciples, the misunderstandings that they entertained of the nature of his vocation. As we have seen, the Messianic secret, that the Son of Man must suffer and die, and on the third day rise again, proved incapable of assimilation even by the Twelve themselves, until it was acted out before their very eyes, and the risen Christ came with his peace to enlighten their understanding. The mystery that surrounded the Passion clothed in a denser veil still the inmost secret of the Godhead of Christ. Only his exaltation in resurrection and ascension taught the Church what had really been revealed. Only in receiving from the crucified and risen Christ the forgiveness of our sins do we discover him to be our Lord and our God.[1]

And so we are in a position to understand the language of Kierkegaard, when he speaks of the divine *incognito*, of the form of the servant which *conceals* the identity of Jesus as much as it reveals it, and of Luther when he speaks of the *deus absconditus,* of the hidden God, as well as of the *deus revelatus,* God revealed. God safeguards his holiness and shows his love in the revelation in Christ, whose glory can only be seen in penitence and in faith. The impenitent can see nothing of the glory of God in the Cross; to them it is a meaningless tragedy, the end of a promising career. But the Church knows God as love just in that very event which for the world stamps Jesus as a failure. If the Cross is the supreme revelation of God, it is so because here the glory is by the mercy of God dimmed till we can gaze on it unscathed, and yet measure its depth by the inexhaustible mystery of the suffering of divine love in the

[1] cf. John 20.28.

51

midst of the evil of the world. The mystery of iniquity is matched by the mystery of suffering love, and God's mercy seen most clearly where he is delivered over to the mercy of us sinners. The Cross shows that God's thoughts are not as our thoughts, nor his ways as our ways. If the wisdom of God is foolishness to men, that is because it so greatly transcends all that passes for wisdom among men. In God's revelation of himself, the mystery of God remains, is indeed immensely deepened, and yet in his mystery he suffers himself to be known.

IV

The People of the Revelation

GOD begins to reveal himself in the history of a people of which Jesus Christ is the consummation and meaning. His acts before the coming of Christ, in calling, liberating, constituting by a Covenant, teaching, exiling, restoring this people, along with his guidance of its tradition, constitute a preparatory revelation. In due time, Jesus Christ himself comes to this people, and enters its history at its turning point. In his own historic actions, he reconstitutes in a New Covenant the people of the revelation, making its basis spiritual rebirth into an international community, where previously it had been natural birth into a single nation.

On his return to heaven, he sends the Holy Spirit to the nucleus of the reconstituted people, to work inwardly in bringing about the knowledge of God in them on the basis of the historic life and death and resurrection of Jesus. The corporate faith of the Apostles, made possible both by the coming of Christ and the new indwelling of the Holy Spirit, is the revealed knowledge of God. As the Apostles of Christ, and the Christian ministry after them, preach the Word of God and administer the Sacraments Christ bequeathed to his Holy Catholic Church, men are called and empowered to share the knowledge of God, as they enter the Spirit-bearing community, and themselves share in the Spirit in the revelation of God. The mission of the Church is now the means of transmitting the revelation, for revelation is relived in entering the Church, the community of the Holy Spirit and the Body of Christ. Thus the Word, the Sacraments and the common life of the Church are organs by which the revelation of God, once mediated in the historic life of Christ, is now again mediated to every succeeding age. Similarly, the liturgy of the Church, the most characteristic point in its life, is the principal means by which the

Church in its own life transmits, sums up, sacramentally enacts, corporately expresses, newly receives and perpetually responds to the revelation of God in Christ.

We have now to explore the meaning of these propositions. First, revelation includes a preparatory stage, also historical in character. In revealing himself in Jesus Christ, God entered history in person. But the Incarnation was far from being God's first contact with history. His act of self-revelation in Jesus Christ was the culmination of a series óf lesser acts of self-revelation, in which he prepared the way for his own coming in person. These earlier acts of his, which together constitute what we may call the preparatory revelation, are the decisive points in the history of a particular people, the people of Israel, chosen to be the people of God, to receive the revelation, both in its preparatory and in its full and final form, and to transmit it to the world. But since the whole meaning of the history of this people lies in its being the preparation for the coming of Christ, we may extend the meaning of the term revelation to include these preparatory acts of God without breaching our fundamental principle that God reveals himself through Jesus Christ.

If God had come to the world in Jesus Christ wholly unannounced and unprepared for he might have gone altogether unrecognized. He very nearly did as it was. Moreover, his teaching would have had no foundation to build on. The preparatory revelation, which is of a piece with the full and personal revelation of God in Christ, enabled him to train a people with an inchoate but genuine knowledge of himself through his past acts, out of whom he could call a few men to be the recipients of the fullness of revelation, and to pass it on to others. The people of Israel, before Christ came, already knew something of the one true and living God. They knew him as the holy and righteous one, the Lord of history, who had acted and would act for the fulfilment of his purposes in history, as the one true God, creator of the whole world and especially of man, as the one who would at the last day assert his sovereignty over his world and bring in an era of perfect peace and righteousness. By a long training they had learned radically to distinguish him from the gods of the peoples around them, to see in his holiness and activity in the world the antithesis of the tribal nature-gods of their neighbours. They knew already of his moral demands, had already been taught by prophets that the knowledge of God is shown in righteous conduct according to his will. They knew already that the Lord is one God, and to be loved, and that they must love their neighbours as themselves.

All this they knew through what God had done in the history of their own people. Their understanding of God was not derived from man's permanent capacity for myth-making, nor from philosophical conclusions from what they knew of the world of nature. On the contrary, all the religious literature of Israel, in which their understanding of God began to take form, dates from after the decisive historical experiences in which God made himself known to them. Whether we date the national existence of Israel from the Exodus or from the call of Abraham, we must still reckon with the fact that Israel originated in an initiative taken by God himself. God speaks, whether to Abraham or to Moses, and from his speaking immense historical consequences follow. The wandering family groups of the patriarchal period, following the Word of God into an unknown future, are the forerunners of the most unusual nation in known history. Israel became a nation, with a life of its own, through the Exodus, through a series of historical events which found their interpreter in Moses, chosen by God to be the mouthpiece of his will to the people, to move them to seize the opportunity of nationhood latent in the events going on around them. The existence of this nation is rooted in their response to the word of God. Without God's speaking to Moses, they would have remained forced labourers in Egypt; the basis of their nationhood lay in the covenant of Mount Sinai in which God himself laid down the conditions on which they should be a people, and that his people.

The later history of Israel brought them equally to grips with the living historical action of God. It was, they well understood, through the will of God and not through their own military strength that they took over the country of Canaan from the inhabitants, and held their position there, whether against the Philistines or against Syria. Later, as they settled down to prosperity and its temptations, they received the warnings of God through the great prophets. The prophets interpreted the life of Israel in the light of the covenant-relationship which constituted it, and so in the light of the Exodus, Israel's redemption into nationhood. If Israel was to remain God's people, and to receive God's blessing, it must keep its own side of the covenant and live in righteousness and holiness, according to the revealed will of God. And so as God acted again through the great historic events of their time, in the invasion first of the Assyrians and then of the Babylonians, Israel knew what God was doing, and recognized his judgement for what it was.

Again, as first one part, then another, of the people was swept off into exile, more prophets interpreted the will of God, and Israel came to know that God's choice of his people remained unrevoked, and that after judgement came forgiveness and restoration for a penitent people that had learned its lesson. Later still, as the promised return of the presence of God with his people delayed, hopes grew up of some new decisive intervention of God in the history of his people, fulfilling what the return from exile had left unfulfilled: some looked forward to a Messiah who would bring in God's kingdom, others to a cataclysmic end of all history as God asserted his sovereignty for himself. And if these hopes had nothing of the historical about them when they were first entertained, yet even these entered into the web of God's dealings with his people, for they provided something of the framework of images and ideas in which Jesus himself and his followers came to understand his mission.

In all these events we are to see a preparatory revelation of God. In them, as in the coming of Christ, God acted in history, revealing not primarily propositions about himself, but himself in action. His mighty hand and his stretched-out arm showed him to be the Lord of history, and as Israel discerned the same hand at work in the history of the nations, as well as in its own, it came to know him as the only God. God, known above all in the Exodus as redeemer, known in history as the only Lord, is recognized as the creator, as the one who made all things by his word. The Exodus faith is pushed back to the beginning of all things. At the same time, through priest and prophet God reveals his will for the people. He interprets for them his mighty acts in history, and shows how he has himself taken the initiative in choosing this people to be his own, and to be the instrument of his self-revelation to the world.

Here again the initiative of God marks off the faith of Israel from all the surrounding religion. The God who chooses Israel is no tribal God, but the Lord of heaven and earth. There is no natural, family relationship between God and Israel. The relationship depends on God's decision: he initiated it, he can terminate it if he wishes. And yet in his faithfulness to his covenant he will not terminate it: he will remain faithful to Israel even if she be unfaithful, as a good husband with an adulterous wife. So Israel, even before the coming of Christ, learned of the faithfulness and love of God, who had chosen Israel out of grace and love, through no merit in Israel, and who would accordingly remain Israel's redeemer through all faithlessness and sin of the people.

All this we find written down in the Old Testament, as the record of God's mighty acts, and the reflection upon them of prophet, priest and wise man. We may believe that just as God provides in a Moses or a Jeremiah the interpreter of his own historic action at the great crises, so he is at work all down the history of Israel, inspiring and moving the various interpreters of his will who compose the books of the Old Testament. There is no doubt much in all this which is merely human, and even some which betrays a wholly inadequate perception of God and his will, yet through it all shines the story of God's preparatory self-revelation, which is seen for what it is when Christ comes, fulfilling all that was true in Israel's life and literature, passing judgement on all that was inadequate or misconceived.

And so in due time Jesus came. When the preparation was complete, God himself entered the life of his people, and took a place within their history, bringing it to its fulfilment in a crisis of judgement and mercy. As the one who is in himself the meaning of all the history of his people, Jesus asserts the true line of its development. To be true to the past of Israel, to Abraham, Isaac and Jacob, to Moses and the prophets, was to go forward with Jesus to the new and fuller understanding of God and his will, to share in the participation he proffered in the Kingdom of God. This was to be 'an Israelite indeed', a true son of Abraham. In the same way, to turn away from Jesus and his teaching and demand was to desert the true line of Israel, to refuse Israel's vocation of sonship to God for the sake of the world. And so the coming of Jesus sets up a crisis in the history of Israel, which ends tragically, in the rejection of Israel. Israel, with the exception of a few individuals, rejects this new stage in its vocation as the people of God, refuses the opportunity to go forward with Jesus into far closer relationship with the God on whom its existence depends.

In consequence, the line of the continuity of the people of God swings away from the nation of Israel into an international and largely Gentile community. But the nucleus of this new form of the people of the revelation is the twelve Apostles of Christ, the patriarchs of the twelve symbolic tribes of the new Israel, the prototypes of the new believing community who find in Jesus the fullness of revelation. The main observable historical consequence of the coming of Jesus into Israel's history is the emergence out of it of the Holy Catholic Church, a Gentile community on Jewish foundations. The old Israel, 'Israel after the flesh', continues, but it is no longer in the same sense the people of God. God preserves Israel in being, but his chosen are those who have faith in Jesus, who live by his redemption. And these may belong to any nation. In their community there is 'neither Jew nor Gentile, male nor female, bond nor free'. All the old barriers and human distinctions of race or status are broken down in the new people of God, for more fundamental than any of these is the unity of those who live by Christ's revelation of God and redemption of the world.

The last of the series of events associated with the coming of Christ happened after his death and resurrection and his return to heaven. From his place at the helm of the universe at the Father's side he sends forth the Holy Spirit, to dwell in the new community, and impart to them the knowledge and love of God which belongs to those who put their trust in the work he did. The old prophecy is fulfilled, that in the New Covenant there will be no need for one to say to another, know the Lord, for (through the Holy Spirit) they shall all know him. The apostolic community becomes the nucleus of the Holy Catholic Church, and now, as they proclaim Jesus to the people, the chain of revelation is for the first time complete. For those who, as a result of the proclamation they have heard, repent and believe, are now baptized into the community of the Church, and themselves come to share in the knowledge of God through the Holy Spirit. The revelation of God, given in Christ, has to be received through the work of the Holy Spirit in the community of the Church.

The revelation of God is not given to isolated individuals, but to the members of a people. God gives his revelation to a people, who are entrusted with the task of propagating it, and the effect of their propagation of the revelation is to enlarge the people by the incorporation of new members into it. Just as God gave his preparatory revelation to the Israelite nation, and offered to them in due time the fullness of revelation, so now the fullness of revelation is received in the apostolic community and those who join it. And this is now so because the community is the community (*koinonia*) of the Holy Spirit. Through the inward working of the Holy Spirit the Apostles and those who with them believe in God as revealed in the life, death and resurrection of Jesus, receive the gift of the knowledge of God. The objective side of revelation is the Incarnation of God and all that happened through it: the subjective side is the presence of the Holy Spirit in the community of believers. The knowledge of God is a corporate reality, into which one enters by repentance, faith and baptism, by becoming a member of the community of faith, the people of the revelation.

Mere belief is already a gift of the Spirit. The capacity simply as an individual to believe that Jesus Christ is the true revelation of God is already the result of the working of God within one. But it is not as individuals that we have the knowledge of God (properly so called). We gain that when we go on to join the Spirit-bearing community of the Church, and to share through the corporate possession of the community by the Spirit in the faith of the Church, which is the revealed knowledge of God. Sacramental membership of the Church brings an illumination beyond the individual's belief in the Gospel preached to him. He must be baptized in order to enter the community of the Holy Spirit. There his inchoate knowledge of God may grow, as he enters more deeply into the life of the Church, as, being a member of the Body of Christ, he comes to share the mind of Christ, and to live in the Spirit, who 'searches the deep things of God'.

Thus the revealed knowledge of God is first found in the world in its fullness in the faith of the Pentecostal community, of the Apostles and others who shared with them in the gift of the Holy Spirit. It was a faith in God revealed in Christ, brought to life in them by the indwelling Spirit of God. The Spirit illuminated for them the meaning of Christ, so that they could see in him nothing less than the fullness of God. They had not yet learned to express in propositions all that they could see in the simple contemplation of faith. Their testimony was simply to the great acts of God in Christ, on the basis of which they themselves believed, and expected others to believe after them. They could not express in words the doctrine of the Trinity or that of the two natures of Christ: but they knew God as Trinity, they knew Christ in his Godhead, as well as in his manhood. By the end of the apostolic age, the Church could express in words propositions which the later Church could recognize as having the meaning that, in more philosophical language, finally came to be expressed in the doctrines of the Trinity and of the Incarnation. But the essence of the Church's Trinitarian and Christological faith was there from the beginning, for it lay in that communion with God revealed in Christ, by the inward working of the Holy Spirit, whose implications for reflection can only be expressed in these doctrines.

There is no development in the essential corporate reality of the Church's relationship with God revealed. As soon as men who believed in Christ entered the community of the Holy Spirit they were brought into a personal relationship with God as complete as it now is or ever will be until Christ returns and all indirectness is at an end. The development which has taken place lies entirely in the sphere of reflection; as we shall see, no such reflection can lead to true doctrine unless it is founded on the original basis of faith in Christ as the personal revelation of God. True doctrine can only be constructed by those who know God in Christ through the Holy Spirit, that is, by those who share in the corporate apostolic faith. How is such faith brought about today?

The Apostles, as we have seen, knew Christ directly, and to know him was to have mediated to them the knowledge of God himself. But even they only came to the fullness of faith after the return of Christ to heaven, and the ending of the Spirit. The full knowledge of God is mediated through the Christ who not only lived, but also died and rose again, and ascended up into heaven. It is on the basis of *memory* of Christ that the Holy Spirit gives the knowledge of God. As St Paul says of the apostolic community: 'Even though we may have known Christ after the flesh, yet we no longer know him in this way.'[1] The knowledge of God is given by the Spirit.

The knowledge of God as the Apostles and eyewitnesses of Christ had it was based on their own memory of all that was important in his earthly career, including his death and resurrection, by which the almighty love of God came most clearly

[1] II Cor. 5.16.

into the view of faith. They could not fully believe until these final events had happened. Indeed, the last of these events, the resurrection and ascension, though we must account them as historical, in the sense that we consider that they actually and physically happened, were not public happenings, open to the view of all. No one was actually present at the resurrection: there is no direct testimony of eyewitnesses to it. The testimony of the Apostles is to the empty tomb and the resurrection appearances, and to the fact that they 'ate and drank with him after he rose from the dead'. It is not clear that all and sundry could have been afforded that opportunity. The common factor uniting those who received resurrection appearances is their destiny as witnesses. There is nothing in all this to deny (what we most firmly assert) a physical resurrection. But here if any-where 'the flesh profiteth nothing, but the Spirit giveth life'. The resurrection is the New Creation, and to apprehend it is to come to belong to it.

Accordingly, the first basis for the transmission of the reve-lation of God is that all the revelatory events should have happened and that they should be testified to by authorized witnesses. This testimony to the revelatory events is the apostolic proclamation (*kerygma*), and that which is pro-claimed is called the Word of God, because it is testimony to Jesus Christ, the Word Incarnate, or the Gospel, the good news of the love of God in action. The Word must be pro-claimed by those who are authorized to do so—that is, by the Apostles, who were themselves eyewitnesses of the Word, and by their successors, who bear witness on the basis of the apostolic testimony and their own verification of it, as they have come to stand in the place of faith where the Apostles stood before them, and themselves to share in the corporate gift of the knowledge of God. This proclamation is made in obedience to the command of Christ, who directed that testi-mony should be made to him in all the world. A man does not bear this testimony of his own accord, but in the discharge of a commission given him by Christ, either immediately, if he is one of the first Apostles, or mediately, if he inherits the charge they passed on to their successors. The Church bears testimony to Christ through its authorized spokesmen, its ministry, who have succeeded to the Apostles' charge and stewardship.

The second basis is that the Holy Spirit should go with this obedient proclamation, so that it should be made not in word only but in power. The proclamation of Christ can become revelation for those who hear it only if the Spirit illuminates its meaning for them, and gives them the gift of repentance and faith. A man may hear about Christ, or read of him, many times, and no vital flame of faith be kindled. But then comes an occasion when the Word strikes home, when Christ comes to life, and asserts himself as Lord and God. Then faith begins, and the man is drawn on into the ever-deepening relationship of the knowledge of God. This event, which must always seem miraculous, is the work of the Holy Spirit.

We cannot map and infallibly predict the work of the Spirit. He operates as he will, and blessed are we if we recognize his operation. He does not confine his work to the formal ministry of the Word, to the sermon in church, to the public address of an evangelist. Indeed, it sometimes seems as if in this post-Christian world he prefers to work more quietly, through a man's reading and his thoughts, through his conversations with his friends, sometimes long before there is any contact with the Church itself. Many can tell a story of God's evangelism, seeking the strayed members of his flock and fetching them home to his Church, without the intervention of any organized missionary or evangelistic activity on the part of the churches. But he can only do this because of what we may call the diffused presence of the Word—the knowledge of Christ which is widespread, however thinly, even amongst those who have nothing to do with the life of the Church. Even those conversions which seem independent of any human agency are in the end dependent upon the witness of the Church.

The third basis of the transmission of revelation is the sacramental ministry of the Church. Jesus said, 'Go into all the world and make disciples of all the nations, baptizing them in the name of the Father and of the Son and of the Holy Spirit'. As we have seen, the term of God's revelatory activity is the incorporation of men in the people of the revelation, to share, through the Spirit dwelling in the community, in its corporate knowledge of God. The Sacraments stand along with the Word as the necessary preconditions of life in the believing community. Through them Christ and the Spirit make new men and give them to share in the new creation, which is the Body of Christ and the community of the Holy Spirit.

It is not enough that the revelation should be given in word, it must be given also in deed. Men must not only hear of Christ, but come into actual encounter with his redemptive work. We know God in the act of being redeemed, in the act of being delivered from our sins and set in the community of forgiven sinners in the Church. And for this Sacrament as well as Word is necessary. Not that the Word is without power— how could it be if it has the energy of the Spirit behind it? Nor are the Sacraments incapable of speaking symbolically of the action of Christ which they contain. Word and Sacrament go together, for both were willed by Christ as the instruments of his revelation. And both belong in the community of the Church, and have as their immediate purpose the making of churchmen, for it is as churchmen that we share in the knowledge of God.

Thus the mission of the Church is an essential factor in the giving of revelation to the world. If God limited himself, within the conditions of the world he had made, to live in his Incarnation at one point only in space and time, it was necessary for him to make provision for the carrying of the revelation to the rest of the world. God's plan for the salvation of the world depends upon the obedience of the Church in carrying the Gospel 'from Jerusalem even unto the ends of the earth'. The Church is entrusted with a mission which is not optional, but integral to the being of the Church, of its very *esse*. When the Church settles down to enjoy the revelation for herself, and forgets her responsibility to bring it to those outside, she fails to understand the very revelation that she has received. To be the Church is to be entrusted with a mission; the knowledge of God must be shared or lost.

Thus the ministry of the Church, with its apostolic responsibility, and its stewardship of Word and Sacraments, speaks inescapably to the whole Church of its missionary task. Wherever the Church is, wherever there are those who are outside her borders, who do not yet participate in the knowledge of God in the community of the Holy Spirit, she is on a mission, she is sent by God to bear witness, and by Word and Sacrament to draw men into the community of faith. And this mission is itself an essential link in the chain of revelation, for it is the means by which God mediates the knowledge of Christ, as in Christ he mediates the knowledge of himself. Through the mission of the Church men come to hear of Christ and life in him, and unless they hear of him they cannot find in him the revelation of God.

Here again the historical and revealed character of man's knowledge of God comes into clear view. Men simply will not know God if the Christian mission is neglected. No amount of respect for other religions, proper as this may be, no amount of dislike of high-pressure mass evangelism, authentically Christian as such dislike may be, can absolve the Church of her responsibility. Where her grasp of this responsibility is shaky, it is because her grasp of the nature of revelation has also become tenuous, so that she somehow expects men to come to know God by some supposed inner light, or natural perception of him. If mission is unnecessary, so is revelation itself.

In this second stage of the mediation of the knowledge of God, the Church, with its ministry of Word and Sacraments and its common life, fulfils a function analogous to the natural body of Christ. The body is the expression of personality in the world: Christ in his earthly life revealed God through the acts and sufferings of his Body. Similarly, now that he has returned to heaven, the visible body of the Church, with its speech in the Word and its actions in the Sacraments, expresses Christ as he expresses God, in the power of the Holy Spirit. So too, if

E

the Church suffers with Christ, in persecution or martyrdom, she witnesses to Christ crucified and triumphant over death. The fact that it is thus that the Church witnesses implies a reservation which we have to make when we speak of it as the expression of Christ. The Church does not automatically express Christ: rather it is her calling to do so, and for that calling she is equipped with Word and Sacraments, and empowered by the Holy Spirit. But her capacity to fulfil her calling also depends upon the obedience of her members. The Word is not a true word if it departs from the one revelation once given in history: the Sacraments can be administered profanely or indiscriminately: the common life of the Church may degenerate into a human in-group, finding its bond of unity simply in being different from those outside, and indifferent to their salvation. The Church has a human responsibility to respond to the offered grace of being the true Church, the Body of Christ through which he continues to reveal himself to men.

Fortunately, the Church's capacity to be the Body of Christ does not depend upon the faithfulness of her members, but upon the faithfulness of Christ, and upon the Holy Spirit, the Lord, the giver of Life. Any degree of human response in the members of the Church is sufficient for the work of Christ and the Spirit: what God does is never proportional to what we do, even if our co-operation is a *sine qua non* for his activity to become visible in the world. And where the Church is attempting to respond to her calling, and to be the Church, there is no limit to what God may do with her. Her obedience liberates into the world the power of God, and God's power to reveal himself goes far beyond the achievements of his Church in fulfilling the charge laid upon her. So the revelation proceeds, as the Church in every age, as the Body of Christ in the world, carries the knowledge of God in Christ to every country and to every new culture.

Finally, the inner life of the Church herself also depends upon the constant renewal in her members of the revealed knowledge of God by which she lives. As the people of the revelation, the central act of her life will be to enter again and again into the revelation, and to renew herself at the well-springs of the true Light. The liturgy is the great act of the inner life of the Church, in which she presents herself before God revealed, and makes her response to him in the power of the indwelling Spirit. The liturgy is revelation in action, as God speaks to the Church in Word and Sacrament, and the Church joyfully expresses the knowledge of himself he has given in answering praise and adoration.

The liturgy is also the great means by which the Church transmits from generation to generation the knowledge of the revelation. Like so much else in the life of the Church, the liturgy is linked both to the historic Christ and to the ascended Lord. In its basis in the Sacrament of the Eucharist, and in the apostolic and scriptural ground of the preaching, the liturgy is linked to the historic Jesus, whose acts are recorded in the apostolic testimony, who himself bequeathed the Eucharist to the Church as the central act of her being in him. And it is the ascended Lord who by the present activity of the Spirit brings to life the forms he himself gave to the Church, and makes them the means of his living revelation of himself in power.

The traditional words and ceremonies of the Eucharist sum up and dramatically enact the revelation once received. Indeed, the liturgy is the classic and normative expression of the revelation, as it is also the actualization of the corporate knowledge of God which is the basis of the Church. This is the true meaning of *lex orandi, lex credendi*: not that any corruption of the devotional tradition may become part of the received doctrine of the Church, but that the well-springs of theology and doctrine are in the corporate worship of the Church, where the once-for-all Word of God and the age-long tradition of the Church together come to life under the breath of the Spirit, as the redeemed community actually enjoys the true knowledge of God. The liturgy sums up and transmits from generation to generation all that can be expressed of the content of that revelation which actually takes place as the liturgy is celebrated. At the same time, it is the vehicle of the response of the Church as it again and again receives the revelation of God. The aim of the mission of the Church must be to bring the whole world into the liturgy, to make all men see the glory of God revealed, that they may give glory to him through Jesus Christ in the power of the Spirit.

V

The Knowledge of God

As we have now seen, the people of the revelation enjoy the knowledge of God. To accept Christ as God's way to man, to recognize and receive the revelation of himself which God has made in Christ, is to come to know God. We have now to analyse more fully the meaning and implications of this statement, and to try to safeguard it from various misunderstandings and confusions. Our first concern will be to discover the sense in which the term 'to know' is used when God is said to be known. We shall then consider in turn five qualifications of the knowledge of God. First, it is real knowledge, knowledge of the truth: the word is not improperly used, as of feeling or prejudice. Second, and equally important, this knowledge, though real, is indirect and mysterious. It must be spoken of with proper caution and restraint, not confusing what is possible on earth with that which will be enjoyed only in heaven. Third, this knowledge is none the less a personal knowledge of God, who is himself personal. Fourth, such knowledge cannot be had without personal commitment to the God who is revealed in Christ: the knowledge of God is a 'moral' and not merely an 'intellectual' affair. It is part of a personal relationship, and cannot be divided from other aspects of the relationship with God. The conditions of its arising and retention include repentance and obedience, since God reveals himself in the same act in Christ in which he redeems the world. The knowledge of God is part of the salvation which it was the work of Christ to bring, and it is not a detachable part. Fifth, it will follow that the claim that the knowledge of God exists in men cannot be dismissed as irrational or meaningless, though it is not impossible to conclude that the claim, though meaningful, is ill-founded.

1. It will perhaps have already occurred to an alert reader

that when the word 'knowledge' is used in this context it has
an unusual sense. It might have been expected that the words,
'belief' or 'faith', would have been used instead. On the other
hand, if knowledge is after all the appropriate term, it might
again have been expected that we should speak of 'knowledge
that' God exists, or that he is Three in One, rather than 'knowledge of' God himself. We have avoided on the whole the
words 'belief' or 'faith' because they are for our purposes less
precise. Where we have used 'belief', we have tried to keep it
for the sort of statement which begins, 'I believe that' such and
such is the case. It will be evident that such an usage is relevant
to our subject, but it must be distinguished from what we
mean by the knowledge of God. The term 'faith' is a difficult
one, and by no means free from ambiguities, some of which
derive from variations in the sense in which it is used by the
different New Testament writers. For the unbeliever, it is a
debased word, and can hardly convey the sense we require.
'Knowledge', though also not without ambiguities, conveys
better, by its very unexpectedness, the strong sense we need.
Its ambiguities are not of an order that we cannot hope to
clear up.

These ambiguities are related to those which we find in the
word 'faith'. They have been the source of much controversy
amongst Christians, and it cannot be said that the controversy
has come to an end. Faith was one of the watchwords of the
Reformation, and one of the divisions between Roman Catholics and Protestants lies in a different use of the word faith.
Each of these uses is biblical. The Reformers based their usage
on that of St Paul, for whom faith is so rich a word that it
seems sometimes to include the whole of man's response to
God, involving in its complex of meaning not merely belief but
obedience, trust and love. Indeed, we might well define what
the theologians call 'Pauline faith' as the response called forth
from man by the whole act of God in Christ, the derived knowledge and responsive love of man for the God disclosed on the
Cross. St James, on the other hand, uses 'faith', with its cognate 'to believe' (the stem is the same in Greek) in a more

restricted sense. For St James, faith is something possible even to the demons. They, like us, know that God is. Thus in a Jacobean usage, faith, or belief, is sharply distinguished from any consequent action, or 'works'. It is therefore not surprising that St James denies that justification is by faith alone, as he understands the word, or that he has been followed in this by many Christians, including most Roman Catholic theologians. But their arguments do not really meet those of St Paul or of those Christians, including most orthodox Protestants, who use the word 'faith' in a richer sense. These observations do not of course take us very far in settling the controversy about the means of our justification. But that is not our purpose. We are concerned to introduce a discussion of the corresponding ambiguities in the word 'knowledge'.

If we take 'faith' in a Pauline sense, as, with certain reservations, the present writer is inclined to do, on the ground that this sense is more typical of biblical usage as a whole, 'knowledge' is an element in faith. If we prefer the Jacobean sense of 'faith', 'knowledge', as we use it in this chapter and elsewhere, is the wider and richer term. We are therefore using 'knowledge', in a richer sense, again, than when we say 'I know that such and such is the case'. As we shall see, when we say that we know God, we mean that we have personal knowledge of him, although this personal knowledge is not a direct knowledge by acquaintance, but an indirect one through revelation. We might define knowledge, as the word is here used, to mean a mediated personal knowledge on the basis of a historical revelation. The distinction we are making is parallel to that found in the Johannine usage of the word 'believe' (again cognate with 'faith'), where believing in, or believing on (*pisteuein eis*) is distinguished from believing that (*pisteuein hoti*). To make such a distinction offers a possibility of reconciling the divergent concerns of those who prefer one usage to another.

Thus, there can be no personal knowledge of God (*pistis eis*) except on the basis of the belief that certain propositions are true (*pistis hoti*). These propositions, which are roughly those

71

of the Creed, or at least those which are the core of the Creed, are bound up with the historical act of God in revealing himself in Christ. Nevertheless, these propositions are not themselves the revelation. What is revealed is not propositions but the mystery of God. The propositions are inseparably connected with the revelation, and indeed are its vehicle for us. Thus they have to be believed with the mind as a condition of the personal act of commitment to the God believed which, along with its sacramental concomitants in Christian initiation, brings us into the corporate reality of the knowledge of God. It is indeed possible to believe that the propositions of the Creed are as a matter of fact true, without recognizing that any action need arise from this belief. It is this possibility which St James has in mind when he insists on the necessity of works. What we are concerned to deny is that such belief can be identified with the knowledge of God. To know that God exists is not to know God. We have already argued this in asserting that a demonstration of God's existence, even if it were possible, would not constitute knowledge of God, and that that knowledge is derived solely from revelation. A knowledge of God which did not issue in some degree of penitence and obedience would not, according to a long line of biblical writers from the prophets to St John, deserve the name of knowledge.

Thus, while we do not equate knowledge and obedience or love, or include these latter acts within the act of faith, we do regard the act of faith as commitment to a personal relationship, which involves at least the willingness to be taught to love and obey. The knowledge of God is a growing reality for those who thus believe and seek to obey, who walk with God, living the life of faith. It is these whose faith, like Abraham's, is counted to them for righteousness, for it vivifies their works, making them the works of grace, the works of Christ who dwells in their hearts by faith.

We are now in a better position to approach, without too great a risk of confusion, the first qualification of the knowledge of God, in which we assert that it is real knowledge, i.e.

knowledge of the truth. When we know God, we are not merely experiencing some subjective feeling, without any objective basis, nor are we clinging to some prejudice or 'dogma' (in the secular and not the Christian sense) which for some psychological reason we cannot afford to abandon. Or at least, we are not necessarily doing so, for it is possible in a fallen world, where the Church also consists of sinners, for the knowledge of God to be impure or to become corrupted. In essence, the Christian's knowledge of God is genuine knowledge, and bears upon objective truth. This is so because it is based on nothing else but revelation, upon God's act of self-disclosure in Christ. God cannot lie or conceal the truth from us, for he is the truth. To know him is to know the truth.

Nevertheless, this is a startling claim, if we rightly understand its implications. There is nothing obvious about knowing God, and those who shrink from the use of such strong language are not mistaken in seeing its dangers. Though it might seem to be obvious, that if God has disclosed himself by a revelation, we can know him, we must not forget what has already been said about the holiness of God, which sets him far above what the human mind can think. No man has seen God at any time, says St John, but the only begotten Son, who dwells in the bosom of the Father, he has made him known. Only the mediation afforded by revelation makes the knowledge of God possible.

Thus it is not surprising that we find, both outside and within Christianity, views of revelation which stop short of this tremendous claim that God has made *himself* known. There is the Islamic understanding of revelation, in which the revelation made to the prophet does not in any degree involve the drawing away of the veil of holiness and mystery from the transcendent and unique God himself. Islam offers to the believer only certain propositions, in themselves held to be inspired and infallible, but most emphatically not God. The believer in Islam knows the propositions set out in the Koran. He does not know God. There are parallels to this Islamic view in the convictions of many Christians. There are those whose concern is so exclusively for the truth of biblical or doctrinal propositions that they believe in inspired words, and seem to be unable to believe in God himself except as contained in these precise propositions. Such a view, whether Catholic or Protestant, seems to miss something of the fullness of the divine gift in the Gospel, in which God offers us nothing less than himself.

A similar shrinking from the full implications of Christianity is to be discerned in those who affirm that God must be more than he has shown himself to us to be. On this view, God in heaven is far greater, and indeed, conceivably other than God revealed in Christ. Those who hold it wish by doing so to honour God and to safeguard his transcendent mystery. But the effect of their contention is that God is not truly revealed at all. For God cannot be divided into parts. If he gives himself, he does so wholly. If he acts, he does so with all that he is. If, therefore, he reveals himself, he does not reveal a part of himself, but is wholly present in his self-revelation. He thus offers us a knowledge of absolute truth, the truth that is identical with himself. It seems that what is true in the contention of these thinkers is best safeguarded, not by the suggestion that God does not wholly reveal himself, but by the recognition that he does so in such a way as to preserve his own mystery. God is revealed in the humility of the Cross, in the reserve of the keeping of the Messianic secret. We know him under the conditions of time and space, by Word and Sacrament and in the Body, which is also a body of sinners. But it is God that we know. He will never be other than what we now know him to be.

Also mistaken, as it seems to us, is the contention, at times popular with Christian apologists, and now more common with the opponents of Christianity, that Christianity is a hypothesis. Here again we are dealing with a view of revelation—if indeed such a view can make room for the idea of revelation at all—which removes God from us, and substitutes for him an idea. And in this case the idea, so far from being the revelation of God, is subject to revision in the light of

74

further experience, and that presumably of the world, which the hypothesis seeks to explain, and not of God. For it might be appropriate to say that Christianity is a hypothesis about the whole nature of God, based upon a partial experience of his action. In this sense it could be correct to say that the theology of the Old Testament is hypothetical, because it is based only on the preparatory revelation. When the full revelation comes, the hypothesis will have to be revised, though what is true in it will stand. However, according to our understanding of the matter, the word 'revelation' is stretched in meaning when applied to the Old Testament, for though it is true that God there encounters men in his actions in history, as he does in Jesus Christ, he does not give himself wholly as he does in the revelation proper. Moreover, when we encounter the suggestion that Christianity is a hypothesis, the implication usually is, as we shall see in a later section, that God and his nature is the hypothesis we invoke to see if it will explain the facts of human life. We start, therefore, from no knowledge of God at all, and all our knowledge of him is inferential.

In contrast to all these views, the main line of historic Christianity has always affirmed that revelation affords us knowledge of God. St Thomas, for example, points out that even when our act of belief is directed in the first instance to the Creed, or in general the teaching of the Church, it passes beyond the propositions believed to the one to whom the propositions refer, to the person of God himself. In making this kind of affirmation, historic Christianity has been well aware of the magnitude of its claim. Thus it has always made it clear that such knowledge must lie wholly in the gift of God. In Catholic language, faith is a supernatural act, an infused virtue of the intellect. It is not even in the power of the unaided human mind to receive a revelation when it occurs.

In accepting Christ at his own valuation, in acknowledging him to be God of God, as the Church says of him, the believer is introduced into a situation in which a growing knowledge of God is open to him. No doubt, if we take a man who has no previous contact with the Church, the knowledge with which he begins is small. He could express his knowledge in a very few statements—he might not yet be able to give personal assent to the whole of the Creed. He knows that God is his Lord, he knows that he is his maker and the one to whom he owes the beginnings of a new life. But even at this level it is true to say that his knowledge goes beyond what he can express in such statements, and that he has been grasped by the living God, and brought into personal relationship with him. He knows the Lord, he does not merely know that such and such is true.

Once a man begins to look to Jesus Christ for his knowledge of God, he has before him inexhaustible resources. As we have seen, everything in Christ is revelation. Meditation upon the life of Christ brings a continually growing apprehension of the nature of God. Nor is it only through meditation that knowledge builds up. As the believer endeavours to reorganize his life about his new-found centre, he experiences the guidance and grace of God, and learns something of his ways. This illuminates his meditation, as his meditation in turn guides and shapes his action. Again, life in the Church tells us of God, as we experience his Fatherhood in the pastoral care of the ministry, and the Brotherhood of Christ in the love of our fellow Christians. This can only be so because the Church is indeed the Body of Christ, the medium of his present self-expression. And knowledge of Christ is knowledge of God, because Christ is personally God as well as our fellow man.

The first reason why revelation affords knowledge of God is, as we now see, that the relationship with a man which God sets up by revealing himself to him, and by illuminating that man's mind so that he can receive the revelation, does not stop short at anything less than knowledge. Because Christ is in a position to give knowledge, as he would not be if he were some lesser being than the Son of God, man finds himself in a position to receive this knowledge. He knows the true God as he is, and not some lesser object, even if that object were a true description of God. Though man's mind is equipped only to know things in this world, God has by the Incarnation made the knowledge of himself accessible on the level of this world. The unknowable consents to be known, but in being known he does not hold anything back. He is wholly present in Christ, for Christ is of one substance with the Father, and so his gift of the knowledge of himself is full, though human in form. There is nothing defective in Christ's imaging of God.

This is what is meant by saying that the Christian faith is true. We must not shrink from this bold claim. If the Christian faith were merely our own opinion, we should have no right to claim for it more than the authority of our own personal insights. We could not claim for it a unique status. But for the revelation of God we must claim nothing less than uniqueness and truth—absolute truth, if we wish to put things that way. Only by that, as we shall see, we mean a particular kind of truth. We do not, or ought not to, mean that the propositions in which we express our knowledge of God are, considered simply as propositions, infallibly true. The truth of the Christian faith, in this final and unique sense, does not attach to our credal propositions, but to the personal truth they endeavour, not wholly unsuccessfully, to express. Truth, as the Christian knows, is a person, Jesus Christ; he is the truth itself, since he is the Word made flesh, God in humanity. To know him is to know the truth, to live by him is to do the truth. Our claim to the truth of our faith is a claim that Jesus Christ fully mediates the knowledge of God, and that no qualifications can be made to this statement, so far as the giving of the knowledge is concerned.

Secondly, it follows that our knowledge of God is not some irrational feeling that springs up in us, which by its intensity or unexpectedness creates in us a conviction of its own signifi-cance, such that we call it our faith. No doubt there are such experiences, in the realm of poetry or painting, perhaps, or in our awareness of nature. Such convictions can be valuable, indeed they may be determinative for the course of a man's life. But they are not the truth. There may be a truth in the poetic or artistic expression of such an experience, but this is truth of a relative order. We are not at such points up against the ultimate truth of everything, as we are in the presence of Jesus Christ. Knowledge certainly implies a rational element, and those who think of the Christian faith as non-rational or even anti-rational gravely misunderstand it. The Christian should feel more at home with the rationalist sceptic than with the believer so-called who deliberately bases his belief on uncriticized experience, on some sudden feeling or conviction which has come to him, and exalts 'simple faith' in a manner which ultimately involves the denial of the place of intellect in his relationship with God. The perverse anti-intellectualism of such a believer can mean in the end that he does not know the true God, but an idol.

Again, it must follow that the Christian faith is knowledge as opposed to prejudice. We do not believe in God through Christ simply because we want to, and are impervious to any of the arguments against our conviction. Our faith could not be called knowledge if we held it against all reason merely because we thought it helpful to do so. Indeed, such a faith would more properly be called a form of dishonesty. We must be prepared to submit our faith to whatever rational criticism may be appropriate to it, and if necessary to alter what we have to say to meet such criticism. Only not all criticism is appropriate, and much of controversy between believers and unbelievers shows that the believers have failed to make clear to the unbelievers the precise nature of what they are affirming, and the grounds on which they affirm it. That there are such grounds, and that they are not such as many suppose them to be, will be clear to anyone who has accepted the argument of this book. The knowledge of God will be more fully defended against irrationality in a later section of this chapter.

2. It is now time to turn to the second of our affirmations about the knowledge of God by revelation. As we continue to affirm in a variety of ways that our faith is knowledge, since God is truly revealed, we are in danger of giving a false impression, of seeming, at least, to have gone too far, of insinuating that we have got God in our pocket, that we have him taped.

Many Christians do give this impression, perhaps through insufficient care in the language they use, more than through actual error in the form of their own faith. We must remind ourselves that the knowledge of God is indirect and mysterious; the believer does not enjoy the beatific vision. We must speak of the knowledge of God with all proper sobriety and caution, following the example of St Paul, who preferred to speak of being known by God. We must not give the impression that knowing God means the same thing as knowing the members of one's own family, or one's most intimate friends, though, as we shall see, it does resemble that in important ways. Christians do not hear voices or see visions when they come to know God.

Much harm has been done to our understanding of the knowledge of God by the habit of many Christians of taking St Paul's conversion as normative. Phrases such as 'seeing the light' presumably derive from St Paul's experience, and we somehow expect that a genuine conversion today will involve some brilliantly clear vision of God or Christ, or some voice which addresses us in the words of God. But properly speaking St Paul's experience was not simply a conversion, but the gift of a resurrection appearance out of due time, and as such doubly unique. When a man today comes to know God by his revelation in Christ, he has no right to expect some wonderful mystical experience, whereby he sees God as the blessed do in heaven. He has indeed knowledge, even certainty, but this knowledge and certainty are of an obscure and dark kind. A man may misinterpret what he has, and because he has been taught to expect something spectacular, fail to realize that he already has the gift of faith.

What is fundamental here is the paradoxical fact, noticed in Chapter III, that the *deus revelatus*, the God revealed, is at the same time, and precisely in being revealed, the *deus absconditus*, the hidden God. God does not so reveal himself that we cannot escape the knowledge of him, for that would be the day of judgement. We should then have no chance of repenting and believing, we should simply stand condemned for our unbelief

79

and disobedience. God gives himself to us in his Word under the form of the servant, in humiliation, in the Cross, and not yet in glory, as he will at the Second Coming. Faith is still a decision which might not have been taken and not the acceptance of the inescapable. Those who speak otherwise are pushing metaphor beyond its proper limits, or basing their faith on a passing emotional experience. The Bible asserts this indirectness of faith by drawing our attention to the fact that we live in a time before the final revelation of Christ in glory, when we see 'in a glass, darkly', and not 'face to face'. It is said of the pure in heart that they *shall* see God, not that they *do* see him. Faith is accordingly opposed to sight, for 'no man has seen God at any time'. I do not now 'know as I have been known'.

The act of faith is directed towards God as revealed in Jesus Christ, and that means, as we have seen earlier, that it is directed towards one who appears in humiliation, and not in glory, whose divine nature is shrouded in mystery. We preach Christ crucified, to the Jews a stumbling block, to the Greeks foolishness. This means not only that our faith in God is an indirect relationship, because it is mediated through the incarnate Christ, but also that the circumstances of the Incarnation itself preclude any exaggerated language about the clarity of our knowledge. That is why our knowledge of God takes the form of faith. We cannot prove our faith in God by an argument that only a stupid man would be able to reject. Faith is neither proof nor sight, and yet in its own right it is knowledge of the truth, since it is directed to God's final Word, Jesus Christ.

Faith may be more or less full, informed or instructed; in certain people it receives a mystical development which is an extraordinary gift; this gift gives a far deeper certainty of God and capacity to recognize his action than Christians who have not this gift ever receive. Nevertheless, there is nothing beyond faith in this life, and in the next there is only the beatific vision itself. The gift of faith, for all its indirectness, even in its mystical development, is closer to the beatific vision than it is to the darkness of ignorance of God, for its basis is the coming to humanity of the one in whom even in heaven we shall see God. The Christ of the Second Coming, of the final revelation at the end of the world, will not be other than the one who walked the roads of Galilee and was crucified on Calvary, the one whom we know today in Word and Sacrament, in the life of the Church and in our meditation upon the Gospel story.

3. The knowledge of God by revelation is knowledge of a special kind. Strictly speaking, there is no other case of such knowledge; only God is known by revelation. Nevertheless, revelation is not so unique that one facet or other of it cannot be illustrated from the way in which we know the realities of this world. Notably, our knowledge of other persons can tell us much that is important about the way in which we know God, for though we do not know them by revelation, we do know them, or some of them, personally, and this is analogical with an important aspect of the way in which we know God. Aspects of personal relationship which we already understand, or to which our attention can be drawn, afford significant illustrations of our relationship with God. They can help us to understand how our relationship to God arises and is maintained, and how it can be justifiable to commit oneself to faith in God. At the same time it is important to remember, as it always is when we are dealing, in a broad or a precise sense, with analogies, that there are differences as well as resemblances between the two forms of knowledge, and that the differences are at least as significant as the resemblances.

We may best approach a discussion of personal knowledge by beginning to consider simpler forms of knowledge. Without entering into philosophical analysis of the theory of knowledge we shall presume, with the plain man, that we have knowledge of what is other than ourselves. The most obvious kind of knowledge is sensory. We suppose that by our five senses we have a direct acquaintance with some of the realities that surround us. I look down as I sit writing, and see the arm of my chair. I observe its smooth shiny brown surface, as it curves towards my hand, beneath my arm. I recognize it as what experience and instruction have taught me to call a piece of polished wood. I touch it, and suppose myself to be confirming that it is really there, and what I had supposed it to be. If I knock upon it, I can hear it. If I wished, I could probably smell and taste it. This sort of knowledge is by no means as simple as it looks, but it is simple compared with the kinds of knowledge we are about to consider.

If I wish to know my chair more exhaustively, I shall have to criticize my sense knowledge, and call into play my reasoning mind. A few simple experiments will tell me something of the inner structure of the wood. To discover much more about it I must either become a scientist myself or call in the aid of one. None of us doubts nowadays that the complete answer to the question, What is that under my arm? will include the assertion that it is a structure composed of atoms, organized into molecules and in their turn composed of smaller particles of various kinds. We have no direct sense experience of atoms. The extension of the senses by instruments such as the electron or ion microscope, which can give on the screen a visual image of the arrangement of atoms, does not provide the same direct experience as we naturally suppose our senses afford. Yet I am at least as sure of the existence of these atoms as I am of the piece of polished wood of which they are components.

Why are we so sure of the existence of atoms, even if we have never 'seen' one? The answer lies in the very precise tool for the extension of knowledge beyond what our senses afford, which we call scientific method. Scientific method, with its combination of precise observation, helped out by instruments devised for the purpose, rigorously checked inference, and repeated experiments, enormously extends the scope of what we can know. The knowledge it offers is of a singularly public kind, since anyone with sufficient training and instruments can repeat the experiments for himself and verify the contentions of the original researcher. Moreover, since the discoveries of science have often a practical application, its results are brought strikingly within the purview of the layman; from plastics to penicillin, from television to the atomic bomb, he is continually experiencing in his own life the verification of scientific theories and scientific method. It is this sort of verification, as well as the more precise sort, constantly repeated over the widest field, which gives science its enormous and well-justified prestige as a way of knowledge. Scientific knowledge can tell us so much that we come to expect it to tell us everything, and to suppose that what science doesn't know isn't knowledge.

Nevertheless, there is at least one very important kind of knowledge which we all have in some degree, and do not gain through science, and that is our knowledge of other people. Our knowledge of persons is not to be sharply separated from the two kinds of knowledge we have already considered. We certainly know others through our senses. It is through our senses that we experience all their behaviour. If there is such a thing as telepathy, it does not seem to afford a means of voluntary communication. None the less, sense knowledge alone does not bring us into personal relationship with others. If I attend a public meeting, I see and hear the speaker, but I cannot be said to *know* him, in the sense in which we use the word when referring to personal relationship. There are many relationships in life in which we are aware of other people through our senses, and still have no personal knowledge of them.

Again, it is possible to have a certain amount of scientific knowledge of others without necessarily having personal knowledge of them. The science of biology, economics, sociology, anthropology and psychology will tell us a great deal about how others, or even we ourselves, behave. We may also use them to gain a more precise and helpful knowledge of a particular individual. But while such an approach is not incompatible with personal knowledge, it does not in itself bring it about. In a simpler way, we may use an inferential or quasi-scientific type of reasoning to conclude that when another person behaves in a similar way to myself, he probably feels much as I do when I behave like that. But in neither case have we reached what is generally acknowledged to be *knowing* that person.

All inferential knowledge is at one remove. Unlike sense knowledge, which somehow appears to give direct acquaintance with the object, inferential knowledge gives us an idea, which we can apply. Scientific knowledge is knowledge of laws. It can tell us a good deal about an individual at points where his behaviour exemplifies some law of which we may have knowledge, but nothing about what is unique to that individual. And every individual is in many respects unique. I do not know the individual until I know him in his uniqueness, and this is what matters for personal relationships.

I once had an acquaintance, a scientifically trained researcher, who thought he could apply scientific method to the problem of choosing a wife. He made a list of desirable qualities in a wife, and allotted scores for each, no doubt suitably weighted. The favoured candidate, he thought, ought to be the one with the highest total score. He applied his tests to all his rather numerous group of female acquaintances, and began to assess the results. He could not understand why it was that several of the women with the highest scores made no personal appeal to him at all, while he liked or even loved those with much lower scores. My friend may at that time at least have been lacking in common sense (I am told he is now married, so there is reason to hope he made his decision in the end by more appropriate methods), but he certainly reflected in a striking form a very widespread point of view, which when applied to the knowledge of God leads to equally disastrous conclusions.

Historical knowledge, unlike scientific knowledge, can bear upon individuals in their uniqueness. Even so, because it is inferential, it is, like scientific knowledge, indirect, and so not yet personal. Personal knowledge can only be had in relationship. I cannot personally know another unless we are prepared to enter into relationship with one another, with all the risks that that involves. I cannot in this sense know the other without being myself involved, or even committed. In a scientific approach, even to people, I can stand back in a detached way, and investigate and know more or less as I choose. Though I can as we have seen apply scientific techniques to people, and indeed must sometimes do so, I cannot have a personal relationship with another if I regard him only as an object to be investigated. I may, and often do, have a relationship with another which is sometimes personal and sometimes impersonal, or which has scientific and also personal aspects. But the two are to be distinguished, and have different conditions.

Again, personal relationships cannot be brought about simply by my own choice. Often enough, they arise spontaneously. Sometimes they can be refused by one party or the other to a potential relationship, and in such a case the reserve exercised makes personal knowledge impossible. Sometimes on the other hand a personal relationship can arise almost against the will of those concerned, where the relationship is one of enmity or hatred, rather than of friendship and love. Here too the relationship is profound enough, and personal enough, for the parties to gain a personal knowledge of each other. Perhaps this is because of the ambivalence inherent in all human relationships, plain enough to those of deeper psychological insight, such that hate may conceal love, as much as love may conceal hostility. Indeed, all human relationships are mixed in character, and their character as personal does not depend upon the relationship being one of love or friendship, but simply upon the intensity of the personal involvement which the relationship brings about. For that reason it is not easy to say when a particular relationship becomes personal. And yet we are all aware that the deepest of personal relationships, above all love, can give to those concerned a knowledge of one another that could have come in no other way.

Personal knowledge, so understood, is within the experience of nearly all of us. We know however that it is a mysterious fact, and hard to analyse and explain, and that we are never sure whether we have an actual instance of it or not. Many married people are sure as they could be of the reality of their personal knowledge of one another. None the less, human beings are always capable of surprises, from the apparent

changes of personality which can occur in unusual psychological conditions, to sheer discovery, to which the divorce
courts bear witness, that what had passed for love and knowledge was in fact nothing of the kind, and that the two had
remained separate even in their physical union. Where, however, personal knowledge does exist, it seems to offer an
apparently non-inferential direct acquaintance with the person
known, like that of sense knowledge on another level. Further
analysis undoubtedly reveals elements of gathered experience,
of rational inference, based on sense impressions, and we
should not be wise to conclude that personal knowledge is a
kind of mystical intuition, by-passing the senses to a direct
spiritual acquaintance of one person by another. None the
less, it has often been noticed that personal knowledge is actual
only in the enjoyment of relationship, and that when we turn
away from the direct contemplation of the other in relationship
to speak of them to a third person, we enter a different sphere.

Here the propositional element in our knowledge of the
other is again to the fore, and at once we discover that what
we can express in propositions does not exhaust what we are
aware of knowing, or of having known, in the moment of
relationship. I believe that I know my wife very well. 'I have
the feel' of her personality. Yet I should find it very hard to
describe her character, and would always be conscious of
having failed to convey the essence of what I know of her.
And this is not because I know her badly, but because I know
her well; my knowledge has so simplified itself that it is hard
to avoid the word 'intuitive', unsatisfactory as it may be. A
rich and complex personal relationship comes also to have the
characteristic of great simplicity. Many elements are present
together and somehow combined into a whole which is more
than the sum of any parts of it that analysis may reveal. Propositions may be useful, but they can only point to the experience of knowledge itself.

A full analysis of personal knowledge would be as much out
of place here as one of sensory or inferential knowledge. At the
same time, it has been necessary to spend a certain amount of

time in drawing attention to its existence, for many who have it themselves have never noticed the fact, though they are well enough aware of sensory or scientific knowledge. But once his attention has been fully drawn to it, no reasonable man should be willing to deny the existence of personal knowledge (except on solipsist grounds) or its distinction from other kinds of knowledge. Now our contention is that we have here a model which can help us to understand the knowledge of God by revelation.

We must again remind ourselves of the limitations of any model, illustration or analogy where God is concerned. In all such cases, the differences will be as important as the resemblances, for since God is himself unique, relationship with him will not be one of a class of similar relationships, but at most analogical with one or some other relationships. It is at once apparent, against this background, that God cannot be directly known by any of the means which are appropriate to realities in this world. On the other hand, this does not mean that he cannot be known at all, since we have no other organs of knowledge. It does mean, on the contrary, that God must reveal himself to us by means which include events within the world, and that God must make use of these terrestrial events in order to convey by their means the knowledge of himself. Knowledge by revelation resembles inferential knowledge in being indirect, but it resembles personal knowledge in transcending the propositional and in being linked with relationship.

First of all, the knowledge of God is indirect. God has no body which we could experience with our senses. The world is not his body, and experience of the world, even of the kind known as nature mysticism, does not afford the knowledge of God. Even the Incarnation, which in a real sense did give God a body within this world, did not mean that one could have sensory experience of God. I cannot gain from the world, therefore, a knowledge of God parallel to my knowledge of others through their bodily behaviour. It is true that those who knew Christ on earth could gain knowledge of him

87

through his bodily behaviour, but if the conclusion is drawn that they thereby knew God, it must be said that if they did, they were not necessarily aware of the fact. Indeed, it could be said paradoxically that it was possible even to have personal knowledge of Christ without necessarily having personal knowledge of God, if the commitment of faith had not been made. Nor is this necessarily to invoke a Nestorian Christology but simply to respect the reserve of the Incarnation, which means that Jesus was really human, and not simply the appearance of a man. Judas is surely the case in point, if we doubt this.

For similar reasons, inferential knowledge of God, apart from revelation, is not available to us. God can neither be observed nor experimented upon. He does not fall within any law. We cannot know him by his effects; arguments to show that we can prove either too much or too little. Either the whole world is his effect, if we accept that the notion of causality here implied is a legitimate one, in which case, as the linguistic philosophers will point out to us, since there is no way of showing that things would be otherwise if God did not exist, our language is meaningless. Or, if we do not accept this notion of causality, the world as a whole is not, in any sense that would be useful as a source of inferential knowledge, the effect of God, and so God cannot be inferred from it. If on the other hand, and more correctly, we consider that the special historical events of revelation are the effects of God in the world, these still do not give us the starting point of an inference of the scientific type, for we cannot repeat them or use them for purposes of prediction. Scientific method was not designed for the purpose of knowing God, and it is vain to look for the knowledge of God along such lines.

Indeed, it will follow that the attempt to know God by inference from the world, to demonstrate his existence as the cause of the universe, however we set about it, cannot succeed. Either the arguments employed are not acceptably scientific in form, and contain logical fallacies which can be exposed, or even if they do point to the existence of a God as the ground of the world, do not lead to such a God as Christians know by revelation. Such a 'world-ground' is not necessarily personal, and if he is reached by inference alone, no means of entering into relationship with him is offered. Thus he cannot be known personally, or effect us as persons at all. He 'merely exists'. Much theistic argument closely resembles my friend's 'scientific' way of finding a wife.

Revelation, on the contrary, offers the personal knowledge of God which is needed. If we begin with revelation, we can see at once the reason for the failure of other ways to God. God can never be known by man in the detached way of an experimenter. If I am confronted by the possibility of God, I must decide, either for or against him. For this, more even than all other personal relationships, challenges me, and calls for the deepest involvement. God will never permit me to know him merely at my own will, so that I could evade that challenge. So he comes to me by way of revelation, making clear that he is a person, and that I must accept personal relationship with him in order to have anything to do with him. For me, God is simply not there, even in his revelation, until I am willing to enter personal relationship with him. I must accept at least in principle the demands of the relationship if I am to go on to personal knowledge.

As always, this is true because God has chosen to come to man by way of the Incarnation. He comes to us in Christ crucified and risen, the foolishness of God. God's foolishness, as St Paul says, is indeed wiser than the wisdom of men, the philosophical mysticism of the Greeks which did not lead to knowledge of the true God. It is wiser, for it deals with what is at the root of our failure to know God, our rebellion against his sovereignty, which makes the knowledge of him intolerable until we are willing to repent. God approaches us in Christ personally, addressing us in the whole of our nature, and in the activity of our nature in personal existence. In the person of Jesus we find the knowledge of God. A human person is the medium of the approach of the Divine Trinity to us. In coming to know Jesus, we come to know God, Father, Son and

Holy Spirit. To know God otherwise than personally would mislead us, for it is his very nature to be personal. Christ's human personality images divine personality; nothing less than personality could do that.

None the less, while it is true that our knowledge of God is best described as personal knowledge, it is important for us to grasp the differences, as well as the resemblances, between this form of knowledge and that which we have of our human loved ones and friends. Our relationship with God can never in this life be one of direct acquaintance. Knowledge by revelation is always indirect, even in its mystical development, though this development is only possible because the relationship is indeed personal. As we have seen, even personal knowledge of Jesus Christ did not in itself confer personal knowledge of God. The original disciples resembled ourselves in needing to make a decision of faith, in spite of the presence of God incarnate in their midst. Indeed, as Kierkegaard points out, the act of faith was far more difficult for them than for us, inasmuch as the offence of the Incarnation was far more apparent to them. If we see Christ through the preaching of the Church and through the Bible, instead of directly as our contemporary and friend, then we see him as it were through a lens of faith, through the centuries during which the Church has been accustoming men to the appalling paradox of an incarnate and crucified God.

There is thus in the end no significant difference between the mode of the knowledge of God enjoyed by the original disciples and that of the Church in subsequent generations. If theirs is superficially more direct than ours, then we have the compensation of the support of the tradition of the believing community. In both cases we have to do with a knowledge that is paradoxically both indirect and personal. As Christ used the means of his incarnate life to mediate the knowledge of himself, so he now uses the life of his Body on earth. Yet the historic Incarnation remains throughout the ultimate basis of all the knowledge of God. Our knowledge of God thus begins by hearing the Word in the preaching of the Church, by the

acceptance of propositions. But as we assent to these propositions, and are initiated sacramentally into the life of the
Church, we enter in the Holy Spirit into the corporate enjoyment, along with our fellow-members of the Church, of the
personal knowledge of God, which is mediated to us through
the whole of our Christian life, while and in so far as it continues to be based upon the Word and Sacraments, and to be
lived in the Church.

Thus, through personal relationship with God in the community of faith, our knowledge of him may be expected to
grow and deepen. It will always be more than we can express
in propositions, and in this it will resemble the knowledge we
have of other human persons. On the other hand, it will be
inseparable from the propositions of the Church's faith, which
are both the starting-point and the normative expression of
what we know of God. Both these contrasting aspects of the
knowledge of God derive essentially from the nature of
revelation, as both historical and personal, as the work of God
in his Incarnation.

We have been maintaining throughout this last section that
the knowledge of God is best described as personal. We have
attempted to show that there exists in human life an analogical
form of knowledge, which is the profoundest form of our
knowledge of other people. We have further maintained that
this personal knowledge of others is the best model on which
we can conceive that knowledge of God which arises in the
members of the Church, when they hear the Word, make use
of the Sacraments and join with others in the prayer and action
and corporate life of the Church.

We know God personally because he is himself a person,
and because he has revealed himself as such in Jesus Christ.
Had God taken any other way of making himself known to us,
we should not have been able in the least degree to grasp him
in his transcendent uniqueness. Only the uniqueness, the particularity, as theologians call it, of the Incarnation, could image
the utter uniqueness of the Holy One. But Incarnation involves
humiliation, the form of the servant, the divine Incognito. It

involves on our side the relationship of faith, personal commitment on the basis of the preaching of the Church, a relationship which involves both decision and loyalty on our part. The Incarnation sets an indirectness at the heart of our relationship with God, and to seek to evade that is to forsake what is Christian in our faith.

4. We must now examine more fully the implications of the fact which has been looming progressively larger as the argument has proceeded, that a personal relationship cannot be enjoyed by the detached investigator or spectator. Relationship with God, like all personal relationships, makes demands upon us, and greater demands than any other. To know God is to know the Holy and Righteous One, and we do not truly know him unless we are submitting to being altered by the relationship, so that we ourselves reflect a little the character of the one we know. 'And by this we may be sure that we know him, if we keep his commandments. He who says, "I know him" but disobeys his commandments is a liar, and the truth is not in him.' (I John 2.3-4.) 'He who says he is in the light and hates his brother is in the darkness still.' (I John 2.9.) We cannot therefore begin to know God without some degree of commitment to whatever may prove to be the demands of the relationship on which we enter.

Here is the fundamental reason why a detached, scientific knowledge of God is impossible: such knowledge has no necessary connexion with action, still less with obedience. One can believe that there is a God and draw no conclusions for action at all: one cannot know the living God without being drawn into a way of living whose motive is to glorify the living God by responding as fully as possible to his love. For since God reveals himself to us in Christ as holy love, we can have no genuine contact with him unless we are willing to respond to his personal approach to us by being made holy and loving ourselves. We cannot know God theoretically, and therefore however probable God may come to seem as a result of a chain of reasoning, a step has still to be taken before the knowledge in relationship actually begins. The 'leap of faith' fuses knowledge and obedience, because it is an act of personal commitment.

There is therefore a place for the activity of the will in faith, as well as the intellect. That is why we speak of 'the *act* of faith'. Coming to believe is an act. In it the whole person is in action, mind and will alike. As such, believing is a profoundly moral activity. The New Testament exhortation to those who have been moved by the apostolic testimony is 'repent and believe', not simply, 'have faith'. When we come to the point of believing, we discover that what previously held us back was not so much intellectual difficulties, though these may have played a part, but something much more fundamental, which underlay them and to some extent created them, our dislike of having a Lord. We wish to be the centre of our own world, to judge everything by the way in which it affects us, to see everything through our own eyes. We have no desire to submit to one who is intrinsically above us, who has an absolute claim upon our obedience. Whether we believe that there is a God or not, we know that the idea of God involves this, and however honest we try to be, we are not disinterested on that issue. We may be glad enough to have a 'religion', with the comforts and consolations that it promises; we may not be displeased even at the prospect of having our intellectual problems solved and our emotional security buttressed by a system of authoritarian dogma. But we do not really want a living Lord, who will not serve our ends, to whom we are at all times responsible, and who demands even that we should be free. In the still relevant language of traditional theology, the main obstacle to belief is the sin of pride, and we only come to believe as we repent of it.

Every believer knows this to be true of himself, and yet at the same time, just in so far as he is learning to repent of his own pride, he is unwilling to say it in so many words to the one who does not yet believe. The Church must take seriously the intellectual difficulties of those who do not share her faith, even while she knows that they themselves, if they ever do come to believe, will be the first to confess that it was not these that really held them back. Those who speak of God to others must respect an integrity in them which may be more potential than actual, and yet in so far as it exists must not be violated even in the name of God's revelation. Indeed, it is precisely the existing integrity of the unbeliever in his present thinking which the evangelist must appeal to, for only this can at present lead him to see the interestedness of his own rejection of God.

Nevertheless, from the full standpoint of faith, it must be acknowledged that unbelief, like belief, is no merely theoretical matter, that the unbeliever does not merely consider that there is not a God, but rejects God. But in this context we must be careful to remember that by the unbeliever in the strict sense we mean the one who has been confronted with Jesus Christ and rejected him. There may not be many who have thus been brought to the point of full and serious decision against God in Christ. We are not often faced with the model situation, the paradigmatic case. The great majority of unbelievers have never seriously faced the claims of God. And yet it is true even of them that their failure to investigate and to decide is not uninfluenced by the advantage to themselves of not having a Lord. The paradigmatic case is after all the one which casts the most light on all the rest. Only the believer really understands the roots of unbelief.

There is no room for God in a universe of which I am myself the centre. A God who could take a subordinate place in his own world would be an idol. Until I step down from my place at the centre of my world, I cannot live in the real world, of which God is the centre. And therefore I cannot know God without repenting of my pride, and taking up my true place in the world, under God and with my neighbour. Unless I accept my subordination to him, and dependence on him, God remains shut out from the world I can see. The knowledge of the true God shines down upon us from the meridian. We cannot see God if we expect him to function as a subordinate luminary in an already organized lighting system.

All these moral and spiritual considerations lead up to the apprehension of a massive theological fact, which is the key to the Christian understanding of revelation. God's act of revealing himself is one with his act of reconciling men to himself, of redeeming them from alienation from himself in sin. It is in the Incarnation and the Cross of Jesus that God is known: we sinners cannot know God except as our redeemer. There is no knowledge of God which is not saving knowledge, for salvation means precisely to be brought from the separation from God which sin carries with it into a personal relationship which is both knowledge and love. We cannot divide knowledge from love, nor unbelief from rebellion. If we need reconciliation to God, we need revelation. The two are one. If it be admitted, as all Christians admit, that all men need the redemption which Christ wrought out on the Cross, it must equally be admitted that all men need the revelation which Christ also and at one and the same time gave to the world.

It is this inescapable fact, which is fundamental to Christianity, that forbids us to take the superficially easier and apparently more charitable way of admitting that there is knowledge of God to be had outside the revelation in Christ, whether through the 'natural reason' or through other religions. Such a concession, however much we may desire to make it, in our shrinking from the rigour of a consistently Christian position, really cuts the ground from beneath all that is authentically Christian. For it says that there are some men for whom Christ is not the way to God, who have not fallen sufficiently to need redemption, for whom sin is just an accidental lapse from a fundamentally godly life, who are not, as we are, involved in the destructive power of sin. Christ then becomes, no longer the saviour of the world, but the founder of Western religion, the leader of one cultus or life-wisdom amongst many. And this is not to make a minor adjustment in Christianity, to save it from ignorance and intolerance, but to make of it something *toto coelo* different. The person who rejects Christianity altogether has far clearer insight into its nature than the one who thinks to make such concessions. Doubtless there are mysteries in God's working outside the circle illuminated by the revelation in Christ of which we can say nothing, just because they are outside the sphere of what has been revealed. But saving this always necessary qualification, we must hold fast to the historicity and particularity of the Incarnation. We can neither separate the knowledge of God from the Incarnation, nor separate the Incarnation from its historicity, as do those who speak of knowledge of God through Christ in those who have never heard of Jesus. Indeed, in the last resort, revelation alone reveals the gulf it has itself bridged: when the full light shines, we see how dark it has been till then.

Since what is here said will be regarded even by many Christians as controversial, it will be well to recapitulate briefly the steps which have led us inescapably to this position. There is no detached or theoretical knowledge of God. To know that there is a God may or may not be possible outside revelation. We have seen many grounds for supposing that it is not. But even if such knowledge exists, it is not at all what we mean by knowledge in the context of this book, which endeavours to use the word in its biblical sense. Knowledge of God is personal, not scientific, and can only exist in a personal relationship. Personal relationship with God is for fallen man possible only through the redemptive act of God which liberates man from his alienation from God, rescuing him from unbelief and rebellion at once. It is in the very nature of God that he can only be known in this way, and it is in the very nature of man that he can only know God so. Even if man had never fallen into sin (to use the temporal language of the myth of the Fall) he would still know the unknowable God by the grace of the God who wills to be known. The created cannot know the creator by a 'natural' act. The knowledge of God is a gift twice over, given once at the creation of man, and the second time, after it had been lost, in and by his recreation in the redemptive work of Christ.

That is why faith involves a leap. We cannot know God in advance of grasping the redemption and reconciliation which he offers. There may be, and in fact are, many grounds which the reason can offer to the will to indicate the rationality of the step which has to be taken, but to see the rationality of the step is not to render it inevitable, still less to take it. Only when we actually do take it do we begin to know God, and only by knowing him do we verify that he can be known. If faith is personal relationship with God, it is essentially active. There can be no question of any separation of faith from works. The old controversies about justification, with their discussions about the role of faith *alone*, have obscured the fact, plain to Luther himself, who coined the phrase, that in the practical reality of the Christian life there is no such thing as faith alone. Faith is a principle of action, it is the fountainhead of truly good works, as opposed to what the New Testament calls 'dead works', that is, works done from outside the personal relationship with God, and not in response to his love. As we put the matter in the summary statement at the beginning of this chapter, the knowledge of God belongs in a context of trust and obedience, in short, of faith in the full sense. We cannot begin to have, and we certainly cannot continue to have, a personal relationship with God if we are unwilling to obey him and to be with him in every part of the life of which he is the Lord. The knowledge of God grows in us as we learn his ways in the practical experience of living our lives with him, and in the power of his grace.

5. How then can it be rational to believe, if we are expected to enter upon a course of action which affects our life at its very foundations, for which apparently no sufficient justification can be offered in advance? If faith is an 'existential leap', a venture in which we risk all that we are and have, must it not of necessity be irrational? Is not the account of faith which this book has given the most irrational possible account of it? The answer to these questions is 'No'. Only by so artificially narrowing our definition of rational as to exclude courses of action which the reasonable man takes every day, can we exclude the act of faith from the sphere of the rational. The so-called opposition between faith and reason can only arise if we misconceive both. No *sacrificium intellectus*, or intellectual suicide, is in question or could possibly be relevant. The sacrifice we make, the putting to death of our human pretensions, is not

in the sphere of the intellect but in that of the emotions and the will, or in the intellect only in so far as its functioning has been distorted by them. Indeed, we can only take the step of faith in an intelligent way (the uneducated or even the unintelligent are not precluded from taking it in their own way) if by God's help we persuade our intelligence to function more rigorously and impartially than before.

It is rational to enter upon a course of action which involves personal commitment, even though we cannot be sure in advance that the commitment will bring us what we expect from it. Indeed, it would not be commitment if our action did not involve taking a certain risk, if there were not inherent in it an element of 'for better, for worse'. We cannot know what it is like to be married without taking the vows of matrimony and so committing ourselves to a fellow human being until death do us part. There are no experiments which we can make that would give us any relevant information in advance of commitment. 'Trial marriage', or experimental liaison, can tell us nothing relevant, because it is an experience of a different, because temporary and uncommitted, relationship, whereas mutual commitment is of the essence of marriage. We cannot learn to be parachutists only from jumps made at the end of a cable. There must come a time in the training of the parachutist when he actually lets go and trusts himself to the air suspended only by the parachute. Before that point his knowledge of parachuting is only theoretical. The irrevocable step must actually be taken, whether in parachute jumping or in marriage, if we are to know for ourselves the joys of matrimony or the safety of the parachute.

Matrimony and parachute jumping are only the extreme cases of their respective classes of commitment. In the impersonal sphere, a similar commitment is involved whenever we cross at the traffic lights, use public transport, or submit to a surgical operation. No one would claim that it would be more rational to refrain from these actions until we could assure ourselves by a watertight logical proof that, when we actually did it, it would turn out to be quite safe. Indeed, we should be very irrational and obviously neurotic if we could never face that kind of daily risk. Similarly, in the sphere of personal relationships, to befriend anyone, or to love them, is not irrational, simply because you cannot prove in advance that you will not be disappointed. We do not regard him as sanest and most rational whose anxiety precludes him from genuine relationship with others.

No doubt in all the cases that we have considered, there is something to justify in advance the action contemplated. Both in marriage and in surgery, the human race has corporately accumulated a good deal of experience of success, as well as of failure. We can form in advance a well-grounded opinion of the probable wisdom of the course we think of taking. Nevertheless, the experience of others is not my own, and for me it can have only a relative validity. It may be, it surely is, a relevant factor in predisposing me to take my own decision, but only my own decision admits me to my own experience. In parachuting and in marriage we are usually aware of the leap we are making: we experience in some degree the anxiety that is inseparable from a commitment involving our whole existence. We do not always notice it in the often-repeated and familiar actions of daily life, where less is at stake. But the same kind of rationality is involved in all these, and we meet it again, *mutatis mutandis,* in the sphere of faith.

How then does the rationality of personal commitment operate in the act of faith? Certainly, the commitment of faith resembles the other forms of commitment we have been considering in that it too is grounded upon a preliminary justification. We can offer to ourselves many rational persuasives; to make these clear is the task of apologetics, which shows how faith is not against reason, even in going beyond it, that the claim that God has revealed himself cannot be dismissed out of hand, that the experience of others who have committed themselves to God revealed suggests that they had been brought into contact with a reality.

Above all, what moves to faith is the figure of Jesus himself, seen in the pages of the Gospels, in the teaching of the Church, and in the lives of the saints. But in none of this is there anything rationally conclusive. Such a preliminary examination can only show that faith is not precluded; it could never show that it is the only possible conclusion. It is always possible to reply to the arguments of apologetics, and to offer some alternative explanation of an equally rational kind for all the facts and experiences alleged by the apologist. The sceptic is at this level no more irrational than the believer.

Faith actually begins at the point when the figure of Jesus comes to life, when he is no longer a myth or a dead historical personage, but someone who seems at work in one's mind as much as any contemporary, addressing us in demand and promise, calling for our commitment. If this happens to anyone, it is rational for that person to take the step that seems to be asked for. The step is a 'leap of faith', as much as proposing marriage, or stepping out of an aeroplane supported only by a parachute. It may be taken quite drily, without any help from the emotions, and in spite of grave misgiving, or it may be taken gladly as conviction floods in. But when it happens, and however it happens, the step that is taken is quite different from merely changing one's views, or coming to believe in certain propositions—that the best explanation of the world is that there is a God, or something of that sort, or even that Jesus Christ is the Son of God, though this will be involved in the act of faith. It is rather that this Jesus Christ now seems not only to be the Son of God, but also a real person calling for one's allegiance. The first act of faith is a prayer.

Such an act of commitment is not at all the same thing as the acceptance of a hypothesis on trial. In the act of faith there is no question of trial. The decision is made in advance of any verification, and must be, since no verification is possible until the decision to enter into relationship with God has brought about, on our side at least, the reality of relationship. The attempt to make faith sound scientific has led to many altogether misleading accounts of it. In any case, the Christian faith does not purport in the first instance to be a cosmology, a philosophical or supra-scientific explanation of the world, going beyond what science can offer, but saying essentially the same kind of thing. This at least has been made perfectly clear by recent philosophical discussion. There can be no question of proving or disproving the Christian faith by observation or experiment, and therefore it could not be relevant to adopt the propositions of the Christian faith as hypotheses. They would remain such for ever; no new fact would ever be discovered which would turn the hypothesis into a theory or a law. In the same way, once the Christian faith is really adopted, no fact could ever tell against it. We continue to believe in God, even if evidence is brought against him, as we remain loyal to those we love.[1] For we have become committed to God as a person, whose reality has imposed itself upon us, as the desirability of another as a friend or wife imposes itself upon us.

Such a commitment seems irrational to the uncommitted for two reasons. Firstly, there is one obvious difference between the Christian faith and the parallels we have adduced, and it is an important one. While it may be evident that Christianity exists, as a theory or a way of life, it is not evident that God exists. The leap of faith involved in becoming a Christian involves accepting the existence of God as well as his character. Secondly, it seems irrational to persist in believing that God loves us, whatever the evidence to the contrary which is presented by the evil in the world. It has been maintained in various ways throughout this book that such an analysis of the act of belief as is here offered by the unbeliever is a wrong one. The believer is not saying that the best explanation of the world as we find it is that it is the product of a loving God.

If this proposition purports to be an assertion in the ordinary sense, then, as Professor Flew[2] and others have clearly demonstrated, it fails to assert anything because it also fails to deny anything. No new happening could conceivably disprove the faith of the Christian, as we have noted; if therefore his faith is simply an explanation of the world in which we live, it is

---

[1] cf. H. A. Hodges, *Christianity and the Modern World-View*, pp. 44-8.
[2] e.g. *New Essays in Philosophical Theology*, pp. 96-9.

genuinely meaningless and superfluous, and therefore presumably irrational, in any sense of the word rational, which could seriously be argued for.

It does not, on the other hand, as Mr Hare[1] himself would presumably recognize, bring us on to the ground of Christian faith itself to say with him that religious faith is a *blik*, not an explanation of the world, as we should agree, but a kind of *presupposition*, to use the term employed by Collingwood and Hodges. A presupposition is a conviction of a very high status in the logical structure of thought, for it precedes all evidence or explanation, since it is in the light of our presuppositions that we decide what is or is not evidence; 'without a *blik* there can be no explanation; for it is by our *bliks* that we decide what is and what is not an explanation'.[2] As Collingwood showed, nobody can think without presuppositions; there is nothing irrational about holding them, although they are insusceptible of proof, since they precede evidence—indeed it would be irrational to attempt to do without them.

Presuppositions can be analysed, clarified, criticized, but they cannot be proved or disproved. Holding them can, however, be shown to be justified or unjustified, since they bear upon the world in which we live. Some presuppositions are unfruitful, especially insane ones: others are highly fruitful, such as those which underlie science. Certainly a plausible case can be made out for the suggestion that the propositions of Christian faith have the logical status of presuppositions, which prove justified in practice. But once again this is not the whole of the matter, nor even its core. Behind the propositions is the person: behind the presupposition is the personal commitment.

We shall always find confusion and misunderstanding in the attempt to analyse the Christian faith and to discover its logic if we do not firmly grasp that it is a personal response to God who reveals himself to us as a reality in his holy love, in the act of rescuing us from our sin, which alienates us from him. Thus, from the standpoint of faith we cannot ask first, if God exists, and secondly, if he loves us, and thirdly if these convictions are

---

[1] e.g. *New Essays in Philosophical Theology*, pp. 99-103.   [2] Hare, *loc. cit.*

compatible with the state of the world as we know it. In philosophical discussions with unbelievers the question always seems to assume this form, and it is not surprising that propositions about God become highly mysterious, in no theological sense of the word. Surely the function of our propositions about God is to point to the place at which God may be actually encountered, the place of revelation. If he is actually encountered, his existence, his love, his overcoming of the evil in the world, are met with as one reality.

It is therefore after all the case that Christian propositions assert something. Only what they assert is not an unprovable theory about the world, which would be compatible with all possible states of fact, but, in the first instance, that an opportunity exists of personal relationship with the living God, who is indeed the creator and redeemer of the world. Now this assertion is compatible with all actual facts, but we can easily show that there are theoretical possibilities of its falsification. For this statement is evidently in a sense a contingent proposition. It rests upon the actual fact that God has taken certain steps in history to make himself known to man, above all in the life and death and resurrection of Jesus. If God had not taken these steps, we should be unable to affirm what the Christian faith affirms, though God would still be God. We should not be able to know that he is a loving God and the creator of the world. The believer must say that since the Christian faith is true, it cannot actually be falsified. But if it could *per impossibile* be proved that Jesus Christ had never existed, or indeed that the basic facts about his life which are contained in the creed have no historical warrant, the Christian faith would fall to the ground.

St Paul faces the possibility of the falsification of the Christian faith at the decisive point, when he says: 'If Christ has not been raised, then our preaching is in vain and your faith is in vain. We are even found to be misrepresenting God, because we testified of God that he raised Christ, whom he did not raise if it is true that the dead are not raised. For if the dead are not raised, then Christ has not been raised. If Christ has not

been raised, your faith is futile and you are still in your sins.'
(I Cor. 15.14-17.) St Paul will not admit that the Christian faith
can be held as a metaphysical assertion about the world, unrelated
to the contingent happenings of Christ's death and resurrection. For him, what is basic to the reality of being a Christian, being delivered from sin, rests without qualification on
the resurrection of Christ. Now it is open to anyone to say that
in fact he does not consider that Christ was raised from the
dead, and that therefore Christians are deluding themselves if
they suppose that in any objective sense they have been
delivered from sin. But it is not open to him to say that
Christians purport to assert something whereas in fact they
assert nothing, and that therefore it is meaningless to consider
the question of the truth of the faith.

Now the believer does consider that God raised Christ from
the dead, and he will not be moved from this conviction by
anyone arguing that this is not scientifically possible. He knew
that all the time: of course no law can be demonstrated by
observation and experiment that the dead rise. He believes
that Christ was raised from the dead for the same reasons as
St Paul, because of the testimony of eyewitnesses to the risen
Christ, and because when he believes in the risen Christ he does
find himself delivered from sin. For St Paul's argument is more
complex than at first sight it looks. Though he is prepared to
speak of the possibility of falsification, he is not for an instant
admitting it in fact. What the Corinthians doubt, at this point
in the argument, is not the forgiveness of their sins, but the
resurrection of the dead, and St Paul is using the possibility of
falsification as a *reductio ad absurdum*. Since it is unthinkable that
you are yet in your sins, it is also unthinkable that there is no
resurrection of the dead, for your actual experience of being freed
from sin could not have happened if Christ had not been raised.

The unbelieving philosopher, therefore, may not justly com-
plain of the irrationality of the Christian's faith that in the
redeemed life he is in touch with the living God, though he
may regard that faith as untrue. But precisely in coming to
terms with what is actually asserted to the extent of saying that

it is untrue, the critic acknowledges the meaningfulness of the Christian proposition. The question of whether Christianity is in fact true as well as meaningful is not here under discussion, for we are expounding the Christian doctrine of revelation from the standpoint of faith. Faith depends upon certain contingent historical propositions, and it is the task of the Christian historian and apologist to consider the grounds on which we may rationally believe in the resurrection. But if sufficient grounds exist for an otherwise reasonable man to come to consider that Christ did rise from the dead, then the Christian faith is not irrational, even if it has not been shown to be true. Apologetics cannot show that the Christian faith is true: only revelation can do that, and only to him who repents and believes.

But is there any sense in which the Christian faith may actually be verified, if it can theoretically be falsified? In the last section, we have been all along addressing ourselves to the one question whether the Christian's faith is rational. We have maintained so far that the rationality of the Christian faith is such that it exhibits the logic of personal commitment. Such commitment needs some preliminary justification, such as Christian apologetics provides. But there is no substitute for the actual commitment, for only this brings one into touch with the reality spoken about. On the other hand, if the preliminary justification exists, and the testimony of others who have made the commitment can be shown, as we consider that we have just shown, not to assert something meaningless, the next step, if a further one is to be taken, must of necessity be the leap of commitment.

Now it might not be rational to continue the commitment if in fact it brought one into touch with no reality—though we should have to be very sure that we had actually made the commitment before we could safely assert that we had tried it and found it wanting, and our willingness to become uncommitted again might be evidence that we had not yet genuinely committed ourselves. But if on the other hand we discover through committing ourselves to God revealed in Christ that we actually are delivered from sin, are reconciled with God and our neighbour, find guidance for our lives and the beginnings of the transformation of our characters into the pattern of Christ, it would be rational to conclude that our commitment had been justified, and so to reaffirm it more strongly.

Such is the condition of the believing Christian. Before he actually made the act of faith, he was moved to do so by various apologetic considerations, but above all by the strange attraction of Jesus. But now he has made it, he is able with all humility to say that he knows the one in whom he has believed, that he has found God, or rather has been found by him. Having begun to believe, he continues to do so because he finds his faith justified, and so there is built up in him that loyalty to the God he knows in part which renders him immune to arguments based on the evil in the world, which seem so convincing to the one who does not yet know God in any conscious degree. Though he only in part knows God the believer is sure that what he does not yet know is of a piece with what he does. There is much in the world that he cannot understand, for the Christian faith does not answer all the questions we should like to ask. But he is confident that when at last he knows God, as God now knows him, he will find the resolution of all problems and mysteries in the God who is revealed on the Cross.

At this point the logic of Christian faith begins again to resemble the logic of presuppositions, briefly referred to above. Presuppositions, we recall, cannot be proved or disproved, for they are prior to evidence. Hence the Christian will in his irritating manner and by God's help continue to trust God whatever happens to himself or to those whom he loves. But he will also consider himself justified in doing so because the holding of his presupposition has in fact opened up to him a realm of living and of progress that was closed to him before, and done so in the way that was predicted to him before he embraced it. Christian faith again exhibits its rationality (though of course not necessarily its truth) by being, considered as a presupposition, fruitful.[1]

[1] cf. Hodges, *op. cit.*, pp. 28-9.

We must now draw this lengthy chapter to a close by sum-
ming up briefly the conclusions of this discussion. We have all
along distinguished the question of the rationality of the Christian faith from that of its truth. We assume its truth—theology
is usually written by believers—but we have been concerned
to clarify the sense in which we believe it to be true. An important qualification of truth is rationality, and so we have rejected
any Christian irrationalism, although our faith seeks to depend
wholly upon God's revelation. Our contention has been that
it is rational to believe in God through revelation, and we
might have added, since this conclusion has been implicit in
our discussion, that it is the only rational way to believe,
because revelation is the only appropriate way of knowing
God. But the rationality of belief is not to be confused with
that of science, or even of apologetics. It is the rationality of
personal commitment, and is seen to be rational in the same
way as we consider it rational, or reasonable, to make many
more commonplace acts of commitment. Indeed, a full human
life would be impossible if we did not acknowledge and
practice this kind of rationality.

VI

The Expression of Revelation in Thought

THE knowledge of God, which is essentially personal knowledge enjoyed in relationship, must take form in the mind in thought and reflection, and it is at this level that revelation is expressed in propositions, which have the further function of serving as the starting point of the faith of other and new believers. The normative expression of revelation is to be found in the Apostolic Tradition, in which Christ's authorized interpreters recounted the events of revelation along with their interpretation in the light of the Old Testament Scriptures, i.e. of past events in the history of Israel, of Scriptural images seen to be fulfilled in Christ, and of the eschatological hopes of the people. In the strictest sense, the Apostolic Tradition must mean the handing over of the revelation itself, that is, of personal knowledge of God through the Holy Spirit, indeed, the whole reality of the redeemed life, through the proclamation of the Word, the administration of the Sacraments, and the building-up of men in the corporate life of the Church. But to do this will also involve the handing over of the normative propositions of faith, as they come to be understood in each generation, and of certain authorized sacramental and other practice, both of which derive their authority from the fact that they are judged by the Church to be necessary expressions of the revelation itself.

Thus the Apostolic Tradition, and its handing down in Apostolic Succession, will involve the transmission of authoritative doctrine. The growth of authoritative doctrine as the expression of revelation is to be observed in the New Testament itself, and later tradition is only continuing that process, which began in the apostolic community itself, when it formulates the dogmas of the Trinity and the Incarnation, and develops a theology of the Atonement and the Church. The tradition of the Church, which we here understand as the developing corpus of expressed revelation, is stimulated to new growth above all at points of cultural transplanting.

The Church can exist in many different cultural environments, and its thought and practice will both affect and be affected by the cultures in which it lives. All such cultural embodiments of the revelation are of relative authority only, and are to be distinguished from the revelation itself. Yet making this distinction is a task of supreme difficulty for any one generation in the Church, especially as the revelation itself was first expressed in the thought forms of a particular culture of the ancient world. How far is even this culture relative to the revelation, or must it too be transmitted to every other culture along with the revelation?

From this point of view, the enduring normative position of the New Testament is connected with the fact that it enshrines not only the first and Hebraic cultural expression of the revelation, but also much of the first cultural transplantation of the revelation, in this case into Hellenistic culture. Every culture through which the Church passes leaves its contribution to the permanent intellectual and social heritage of the Church. Tradition is continually enriched by new interpretation of Scripture, yet Scripture retains its normative position, as controlling all subsequent cultural translations. The task of the theologian in every generation is faithfully to expound the original revelation in each new cultural form within which the Church is living, and by doing this within the fellowship of tradition, and in obedience to the norm of the Apostolic Tradition enshrined in Scripture, to expose all developments in the life of the Church to the criticism of the historic revelation itself. At the present time this task will involve participation in the developing theological tradition of the ecumenical movement.

This somewhat lengthy summary defines the next part of our task. Our subject is now the range of problems involved in the fact that of necessity the revelation must be expressed in thought, and therefore in communicable propositions. We have already contended that the truth of revelation does not reside in these propositions considered in themselves, but in the reality of the gift of the knowledge of God in relationship. Nevertheless, if the revelation is to be thought and spoken about, which is a necessity for human beings, it must be mediated at the intellectual level: it cannot remain ineffable, or it could hardly be transmitted. Equally, it is desirable that the task of expressing the revelation in propositional form should be carried out as well as possible. If no single proposition is infallibly true, since the truth of revelation is personal, and it would therefore be a category mistake to claim infallibility for a proposition, none the less some propositions are truer than others, and some are not true at all.

If no propositions are infallible, some are authoritative, and it is to these that we refer when we use the expression, revealed truth, or more strictly, truths of revelation. Once we begin to reflect upon the revelation by which we live, we raise the question of authority. The importance of the question of authority does not lie in the tendency of fallen human nature to seek an idolatrous security, outside the personal relationship with God, in a set of propositions which can never be questioned, but in that propositions have a twofold relationship to the knowledge of God itself: they not only express an existing knowledge and give form to it, but they serve as the starting-point of new knowledge for someone else.

It is not so important if I, as a believer, wrongly express in words to myself the knowledge of God that I have as a forgiven and penitent sinner; it is extremely important if I wrongly describe God to another person who has not yet entered into personal relationships with God. If that person acts upon my wrong description, he may achieve a distorted relationship with the true God, or even a pseudo-relationship with a God who does not exist, except as a powerful force in the person's mind. Indeed, if I belong to a missionary Church, I can never say that my reflection upon my faith is a private matter, about whose accuracy I can be irresponsible, for I may at any time have to speak of God, making use of the propositions that are available to me. In that sense every believer is a theologian, and must learn the theologian's sense of responsibility to the truth, just as every theologian must remember that he is primarily a believer, and never allow his theology to stray too far from his prayer.

Christian propositions, however, have a special character which distinguishes them sharply from the attempt of the mystic to express the inexpressible union with God he enjoys, and this characteristic of Christian propositions makes the task of the (lay or specialist) theologian much easier. All genuinely Christian propositions take their starting-point from the history of Jesus. Our knowledge of God is not such that once we have started from the historical Jesus we can go on to depend only on the present relationship. We cannot leave the historic Jesus behind: he is permanently the mediator of our relationship with God. Though he is a living Lord whom we encounter today, he is still the one who lived within human history in the first century. It is in looking towards, not away from Jesus that we see God, in so far as seeing is in question.

The first Christian propositions are historical ones; they tell the story of Jesus. The apostolic preaching, as the book of Acts explicitly and the rest of the New Testament implicitly tells us, consisted of the recital of the principal events of Jesus' saving work, along with an interpretation of the events in the light of the Old Testament Scriptures. It is always characteristic of Christian faith to express the knowledge of God we have now by reference to what God did then. We simply do not know God or Jesus as our Lord today if we understand him otherwise than as he was in history two thousand years ago. However far Christian theology may develop the doctrine of God—and it may well seem that it sometimes goes an astonishing distance—it must remain strictly under the control of the historic incarnation of God, for this is the source of our knowledge. This is what is meant by the widely held view that theology is essentially Christology. This is not an arbitrary limitation which prevents us from saying anything about creation or the Holy Spirit, but a fruitful one which may serve to prevent us from saying what is untrue when we speak of those realities.

The Christian revelation, therefore, has a normative expression. It is certainly not free speculation. Indeed, the normative expression of revelation is part of the event of revelation itself. This expression is necessarily linked in time to the coming of Jesus into history. Christian thought is always controlled by its beginnings, even though with the passage of time and the accumulation of a corpus of interpretation we may come to understand the revelation at the level of thought better than those who first received it. Nevertheless, if we understand it differently from them, we shall be understanding it wrongly. There is such a thing as heresy, even if there is not such a thing as a revealed proposition having the property of infallibility. The normative expression of the Christian revelation is the Apostolic Tradition, which is embodied in the New Testament. The Church defined the canon of the New Testament in order that for all time it would be possible to know what the Apostles handed over to the Church, and to distinguish that from later reflection on the basis of what they handed over.

The Apostolic Tradition, then, considered from this point of view, is a body of propositions, which express the knowledge of God as it appeared to those who received it at first-hand from Jesus Christ and through the original coming of the Holy Spirit. And these propositions have at their core a group of propositions about Jesus, which are mainly historical, and end in directions to anyone who desires the knowledge of God for himself to repent and be baptized. They are essentially the same ones which are now embodied in the Creeds of the Church. In origin, these propositions seem to have been those agreed by the apostolic community itself as normative and as forming a standard for all Christian proclamation wherever it took place and whoever was the missionary.

St Paul states them very clearly at the beginning of I Cor. 15. 'Now I would remind you, brethren, in what terms I preached to you the gospel, which you received, in which you stand, by which you are saved, if you hold it fast—unless you believed in vain. For I delivered to you as of first importance what I also received, that Christ died for our sins in accordance with the Scriptures, that he was buried, that he was raised on the third day in accordance with the Scriptures, and that he appeared to Cephas, and then to the twelve. Then he appeared to more than five hundred brethren at one time, most of whom are still alive, though some have fallen asleep. Then he appeared to James, then to all the apostles. Last of all, as to one untimely born, he appeared to me. . . . Whether then it was I or they, so we preach and so you believed.' Similar accounts of the basic Apostolic Tradition can be found in other parts of the New Testament, notably, in a somewhat expanded form, in the early speeches of the Apostles to the people in Acts, and the same outline underlies the structure of the Gospels.[1]

We may note that this Apostolic Tradition, which includes the interpretation of the death of Jesus as 'for our sins', and of both death and resurrection as the fulfilment of Scriptural prophecy, antedates the conversion of St Paul: he himself received it before he delivered it to others. It was part of the standard preaching of the Gospel, which every convert would receive as he joined the Church: it had nothing to do with St Paul's personal Gospel, which he received 'by revelation and not from men', which nevertheless agreed in principle with the preaching of those who had been Apostles before him.

St Paul's personal Gospel evidently centred on the idea of the death and resurrection of Christ as reconstituting Israel, so that the people of God were no longer the community of those who by circumcision accepted the Law, but those of every nation who were justified by the free gift of God received by faith and sealed by the Holy Spirit in Baptism. That Gospel caused controversy in the early Church. But there was no controversy about the basic propositions which St Paul understood as implying his Gospel. The saving death and resurrection of Christ as the way out of sin to the knowledge and love of God were believed by the Judaizers as by St Paul, and preached by them as much as by him. Here is a tradition of

[1] cf. C. H. Dodd, *The Apostolic Preaching and its Developments.*

even higher authority in the Church than the writings of St Paul were at first, to which both sides could appeal even in a controversy of such magnitude. If the Church has in the end come to believe that St Paul was right, it has been in the light of the one tradition which he and his opponents both acknowledged.

On this one tradition, with its recital of historical events and Scriptural interpretation, the evangelists and theologians of the New Testament build. Their salvation, their capacity to enjoy the reality of the knowledge and love of God, rests upon their acceptance of these basic propositions and their willingness to act upon them in repentance, faith and membership of the Church. But in so accepting and acting upon them, they come to stand within the apostolic community, and in the power of the indwelling Spirit to understand more deeply the one revelation of God, and so to become witnesses and inspired interpreters of it. Thus, when they expound the revelation more fully in epistles and gospels, drawing upon more of the tradition about Jesus, and thinking out the relation between the act of God in Jesus and his past acts in the history of Israel, and also the present need of man, they come to increase by many times the corpus of authoritative propositions, which swell the Apostolic Tradition, as the Holy Spirit takes the things of Christ and shows them to the Church. The Holy Spirit shows them no new events, unknown before, though more and more of the stories about Jesus become the common possession of the Church. But on the basis of the essential events in the life of Jesus he increases their understanding of God, of his salvation in Jesus and his present will for the Church.

The same core of the tradition was later transmitted in the 'rule of faith' of the early Church, after the end of the apostolic age, and soon began to assume the shape of the early forms of the Creeds. It was in the light of this rule of faith, the direct descendent of the apostolic preaching, that the Church learned to distinguish in the literature about Jesus and the Apostles the authentically apostolic, and so to exclude from what were coming to be recognized as the Scriptures of the New Covenant all that did not faithfully reflect the one Apostolic Tradition. Indeed, unfamiliar as the idea may sound, it cannot be doubted that at this stage the Church judged what was Scripture in the light of tradition. The Church knew what the apostolic Gospel had been, and continued to share in the corporate reality of the saving knowledge of God based upon it, and it was thus and only thus that the Church could distinguish the Scriptures which embodied the Apostolic Tradition from other writings which might claim to be Scripture, which were indeed in some churches read at the liturgy, and so were actually treated as Scripture.

The purpose of canonizing the books of the New Testament, of creating an authoritative body of writings, parallel to and completing the Scriptures of the Old Covenant, was not a preference for Scripture over tradition, for there were some in the early days who professed to prefer tradition, but a preference for true tradition over false. The New Testament books were canonized as true tradition. Nevertheless, they did not supersede the other organs of transmission of tradition, the liturgy above all, the catechetical tradition, the early Creeds. It was the same period in the history of the Church as that in which the New Testament canon was fixed which saw the growth of authoritative creeds, and the tendency to fix the wording of the liturgy, which had previously been left to the prophetic inspiration of the celebrating Bishop.

Nevertheless, in canonizing the books of the New Testament, the Church acknowledged a norm. Here, within a growing body of apostolic tradition, was a nucleus which was genuinely apostolic in origin. Later forms of the tradition might also be apostolic in the sense of being faithful to the Apostles' teaching. But from the first the Church knew of the possibility of doctrinal disputes: indeed one of the bitterest took place between St Paul and the Judaizers in the period before the composition of the New Testament writings. This was a dispute between parties both of which accepted the essential form of the tradition, in the recital of the historic events of

God's saving work in Jesus, along with the key to them as the fulfilment of Scripture. But the Judaizers believed one could only become a Christian by first becoming a Jew, by being circumcized and keeping the law, while St Paul saw that the New Israel in Christ was a community in grace, transcending the old distinction between Jew and Gentile. The canonization of the books of the New Testament, including the Pauline corpus, settled that question for good and all.

On the other hand, it also settled the question raised by Marcion, of the possibility of the Church freeing itself completely from its Jewish origins, and taking the New Testament Gospel straight into the environment of modern thought and spirituality. For the Church canonized not only Paul's, but other epistles, and gospels other than Luke's, both of whom Marcion favoured exclusively; the effect of the additions to Marcion's collection was unequivocally to set the Church and her Gospel in the context of the Old Testament. And the New Testament as a whole was set alongside the Old and the two together acknowledged as the Bible of the Church. This is to say that the way to interpret the apostolic Gospel, which the living Church hands over to you, is in the light of the Old Testament. The authorized interpretation, which is now to be found in the New Testament as a whole, interprets Jesus and his work in the light of the earlier events in the history of God's people, above all the Exodus, which had been as normative for the Old Israel as the death and resurrection of Christ for the New. Jesus is seen as the fulfilment of Old Testament images, prophet, priest, king, sacrificial victim, wisdom of God, word of God, and others. He is also seen as fulfilling the hopes of his people for the final intervention of God in the last days, defeating evil and establishing his own Kingdom for all time.

Thus it remained true that when the Church in later times carried out her mission she confronted the world wherever it would listen with something very like the original preaching of the Apostles, that is, the historical outline, with its minimum of interpretation, which now found a place in her Creed. The knowledge of God is not, in the classical form of the Church's transmission of it, derived from the unprepared-for reading of the New Testament; the New Testament is not put straight into the hands of the enquirer, and indeed could hardly be, before the invention of printing. On the contrary, the knowledge of God is derived from believing in Jesus and in his saving work in a relatively simple way, and from sacramental membership in the community of the Holy Spirit. Thus the Apostolic Tradition must in the strict sense mean the handing over of the living knowledge of God, which comes to men who are liberated from their sins by faith in Jesus crucified and risen, and are baptized into the Church, in which they share in the corporate reality of faith. The role of the Apostolic Tradition is to hand over the revelation itself, and essentially this is done by handing over not merely a group of propositions, but the whole redeemed life. Revelation is transmitted not simply through the Word, but also through the administration of the Sacraments, and in the whole life of the Church as the Body of Christ.

We have throughout been contending that the truth of God is God himself, given by himself to our knowledge through his coming to this world in Jesus Christ. Secondly, we have been contending that the knowledge of God in Jesus Christ is itself mediated to succeeding generations by the preaching of the Word, the administration of the Sacraments, and the common life of the Church in Christ. We have now been contending that the transmission of the knowledge of God, of the revelation, is inseparable from certain propositions, and inevitably generates a whole process of thinking, which originates partly from the experience of revelation itself, partly from the attempt to give these basic propositions a fuller and more precise interpretation. It follows that, although infallibility attaches only to the direct relationship of faith between the believer and God, which he enjoys corporately in the Church, authority of the highest order attaches to those propositions which have from the first been inseparably linked with the transmission of the revelation, and of a somewhat lesser order to those further propositions which fill out and interpret the propositions of the rule of faith.

Thus, even though it is of the first importance to understand the Apostolic Tradition as in the first place the transmission of the living revelation itself, we cannot for a moment ignore the role of the propositional expression of faith in its transmission, and therefore the authority of the propositions by which it is transmitted. We have seen that the Church judged as necessary expressions of the revelation, and therefore as authoritative over her own belief and practice, firstly, the rule of faith, which corresponds on the one hand to the original preaching and tradition of the Apostles, and on the other hand to the later baptismal creeds, in the case of the Western Church what we know today as the Apostles' Creed; secondly, she accepted the books of the New Testament as authoritative, because they represented the Apostolic Tradition itself, in a fuller but none the less original form. Thirdly, she regarded as authoritative her sacramental practice, of which the core was the Eucharistic liturgy, which included the reading of the Scriptures of the Old and New Testaments, as well as the living testimony of the Church to the revelation, given upon their basis. The form of the liturgy itself was certainly, though less precisely, regarded as authoritative, and therefore as a bond of unity between the different sections of the Church, much as the Book of Common Prayer, in all its different forms in different provinces, is regarded as a bond of union by the Anglican communion today.

All these things would be transmitted from generation to generation, and formed part of what we mean, or ought to mean, by the Apostolic Succession. The Apostolic Succession, rightly understood, is the handing over of the whole authentic life of the Church, based on the one historic revelation, from one generation to the next. Thus when the Bishops of one generation solemnly hand on their charge to whose who are to be the Bishops of the next, they are setting their seal, in prayer and in faith, to the fact that all these elements of apostolicity in the Church are indeed truly being transmitted to the

118

oncoming generation, and by their choice (however exercised) of fit persons to succeed them, as well as their solemn ordination or consecration, securing that this shall be the case.

Thus it emerges from this analysis of the Apostolic Tradition that the Church possesses a body of authoritative doctrine, whose foundations lie in the rule of faith, the apostolic proclamation of Jesus, crucified and risen, as Saviour, filled out in Scripture. It is the natural tendency of such a body of doctrine to grow, as more and more minds, from more and more cultural backgrounds, begin to play upon the revelation that has illuminated them. Here lie the most delicate problems in regard to the authority of the Church's faith. Doubtless, the corporate reality of faith brought about by the Holy Spirit in the Church has almost absolute authority over the neophyte. Nevertheless, the very fact of the canonization by the Church of the books of the New Testament implies the possibility of her growing tradition going astray, losing its anchorage in the one historic revelation. Not every proposition which purports to express the one faith is authoritative, and some need to be discarded as the Church comes to think better of them, while others which are put forward from time to time should never be admitted at all, since they cannot be derived from the Christological revelation.

The crucial question the Church has to face, as her body of doctrine grows, is which of these developments are necessary expressions of the revelation itself, as making explicit, in ways which are essential in order to avoid misinterpretation, implications of the basic propositions of faith themselves. Such propositions will attain the status of dogma, which the Church expects never to alter, though she may come to find it desirable to revise their language. Other doctrinal propositions, which relate to elements in the faith of almost or quite equal importance, may not reach dogmatic status, since they never reach such classical precision and simplicity of formulation as to commend themselves to the whole Church. They may nevertheless carry a very high degree of authority, without reaching the final status of being acknowledged by the whole Church as binding. This is the case, for example, with the doctrine of the Atonement, which has no dogmatic formulation, at any rate so far, and yet bears upon a reality which all orthodox Christians would agree is central to the whole faith.

The activity of the theologian, in seeking to express the revelation in doctrinal propositions, is already in evidence in the New Testament itself. We certainly do not find the New Testament writers, and it is not to be supposed that the other apostolic thinkers whom they represent would have differed from them in this, confining themselves to repeating without comment the propositions of the original apostolic proclamation. St Paul, St John, the writer to the Hebrews, are the great theologians of the New Testament. But in another way, every New Testament writer is a theologian, in so far as he thinks about the revelation and seeks to express it truly for the benefit of the Church and its mission. The apostolic community itself already confronted the problems which form the subject matter of later theological reflection, the relationship of Jesus to God, the way in which his death and resurrection saved the believer, the relationship of the Church to Israel and to the Gentile world, the nature of the Christian life. The personal reality of the redeemed life always needs the support of reflection if it is to develop to its full flower even in each individual, let alone to be transmitted in a world in which men rightly confront the Church with searching questions about the meaning of what she says.

Accordingly, when the Church turns to the task of formulating her fundamental doctrines, the Trinity and the Incarnation, and to constructing a theology of the Atonement and the Church and Sacraments, she is not entering upon some new phase of her life, but doing in a more concentrated way what had been part of her task and her activity from the beginning. This is demonstrated by the mere fact that we insist that these doctrines shall be Scriptural if they are to win the assent of the Church. Scripture already contains the basis of these doctrines, in the work of the first generation of Christian thinkers. When the apostolic community took the daring step of calling Jesus 'Lord', an attribution which constituted, according to some present-day scholars, its first credal affirmation, it was already sketching in the first outlines of the doctrine of the Trinity, for the 'Lord' was none other than the divine name, the name which is above every name, belonging to God alone. That step was taken before the first book of the New Testament was written. It seems highly probable that a Trinitarian pattern of speech was already developing at the same period, as is shown in many examples from the letters of St Paul. In these the Holy Spirit is not always co-ordinated with the Father and the Son, as he is in the famous II Cor. 13.14, but St Paul certainly thought of the Holy Spirit as sharing in the divine majesty of the Father and the Son.

As for the Incarnation, even more obviously the data for a developed doctrine are scattered all over the New Testament, and the Church had only to harmonize faithfully the recorded accounts of Jesus' life and teaching about himself, along with the growing thought of the New Testament writers. The divinity and humanity of Jesus are both clearly present to the writer to the Hebrews and to St John, and we can hardly doubt that the same is true of St Paul. But the New Testament writers hardly think of God incarnate except in his activity of revealing himself and reconciling the world to himself. The doctrine of the Incarnation, as it begins to take shape in the New Testament, is part of the doctrine of the Atonement. Here, too, theological activity is manifest. In images drawn both from the Old Testament and the contemporary life of man, the apostolic writers strain language to convey the meaning of Christ's work in dying for our sins in accordance with the Scriptures, and in being raised the third day in accordance with the Scriptures.

A doctrine of the Church had also to be thought out. Clearly the Church from the first thought of itself as Israel, the faithful remnant of the original people of God. But it was not clear from the first how the new and true Israel was related to the old, to 'Israel after the flesh', nor how it was related to the world of the nations outside. Gradually it became clear that the Church was not simply a continuation of the Old

Israel, but intimately a part of the redemptive event itself, the Body of Christ and the Temple of the Holy Spirit, and as such transcended all national barriers, affording to Jews freedom from the burden of the Law, as well as a challenge to cast away the pride of being the people of the Law, and to live with Gentiles by the free grace of God.

Thus tradition in later periods carries on the activity of the first Christian generation, when in the light of the culture then prevalent it asks and answers to its own satisfaction the classical theological questions. The first generation already had engaged in a ferment of theological activity which could never be surpassed for fertility. The expansion of the corpus of authoritative doctrine from the brief and largely factual statements of the apostolic proclamation to the whole body of the New Testament Scriptures could never be paralleled in the future history of the Church. Later generations inherit as authoritative the work of the New Testament authors, and build upon it. In so far as their building is genuinely upon the true foundation of Jesus Christ, the work of every generation in reflection upon the revelation becomes part of the Apostolic Tradition.

We are accustomed, and in a sense rightly, to be suspicious of the development of tradition; we know how it can embroider piously upon a small nucleus of fact, and in the end transform a religion out of all recognition. Without looking any nearer home, we can see this happening in Mahayana Buddhism. We shall do well to be suspicious of any Christian attempt to found doctrine upon events of which there is no record in the New Testament, on the ground that they have been transmitted by oral tradition, or even that it is congruent with the rest of the faith that they should have taken place.

Nevertheless, we cannot allow such suspicions irrelevantly to blind us to the fact that it is inevitable that doctrine should develop and grow, as generation after generation reflects upon the same data. From the perspective of faith, this is simply the fulfilment of Christ's promise that the Holy Spirit should take that which is his and the Father's, and show it to the Church, and so lead us into all truth. We cannot today receive the faith as if the intervening period of tradition had never happened. We must receive as it comes to us from the living Church. This is not to say, as we shall see, that we must accept in every detail what has become traditional in the Church, for Scripture remains normative, but it is to say that we shall greatly and perhaps heretically impoverish our reception of the revelation if we ignore tradition. Indeed, we cannot ignore tradition even if we want to: the very churches which claim to base themselves upon Scripture alone manifestly interpret Scripture in the light of a very rigid and selective tradition of their own. Even the detached historical scholar interprets Scripture in the light of the tradition of biblical scholarship which he inherits, much of which is itself becoming part of the growing Apostolic Tradition of the whole Church.

The Apostolic Tradition, then, in the light of which we interpret the rule of faith and the New Testament, is continually growing. But it does not always grow at the same speed. There are periods of relative stagnation in the life of the Church, when new questions are not being asked, and old answers seem adequate to the Church's needs. Such development as there is consists in the continual refinement of a particular system of ideas, the basis of which comes to be taken for granted as if it were inevitably or self-evidently true, and to be equated with the revelation itself. Such was the Western mediaeval synthesis, until the Renaissance brought new questions which have never been fully answered. Such today is still the position of the majority of the Eastern Orthodox churches, who remain satisfied with the patristic synthesis, as if it were the only possible expression of the faith. The tradition develops speedily, and therefore also dangerously, at periods when the Church is entering and taking root in a new culture.

It has been remarked that Christianity is exceptionally sensitive to its cultural environment. It seems, unlike Hinduism, Buddhism and Islam, which apparently dominate completely the culture around them and make it the product of themselves, to interact with the culture in which it lives. If Europe is the product of Christianity, it is also true that Christianity as we know it in the West is the product of European culture, with its Hellenic and later humanistic elements. We are unaware of the completeness of this cultural identification until we find the culture changing, either because we seek to plant the faith in some new culture, as when the Church in its missionary task goes abroad and finds the cultural challenge of its new environment facing it with questions never before asked, and calling in question so much that had been taken for granted, or because, as in Western Europe today, a culture in which the Church has been long established undergoes obvious and rapid changes, so that the Church is temporarily disadapted to the new culture which is succeeding the old.

We do not find it difficult to understand the relativity of any particular cultural embodiment of Christianity, at least if we stop to think, when it is simply a matter of customs or architecture. Almost anyone can see the unsuitability of building Gothic churches in India or China, though it is less easy to see the unsuitability of doing so in twentieth-century Britain, where existing Gothic churches supply so pleasantly a bolt-hole from the cultural problems of the revolution that is going on around us. Although it is easy to say that the answer at that level in our Western culture is to have architects who believe in the faith of Church and understand the laws of its worship design churches in the same idiom that they would employ for factories and offices, dwelling houses and concert-halls, there is no equally obvious answer in countries where the only alternative model is the temple of an alien and still immensely powerful religion. Nor, if we look more deeply, is it really so clear that we have a short cut to the answer in our own country. For supposing the challenge of the cultural changes in which we are living goes very much deeper, as it almost certainly does, the task of the Christian architect may be insoluble until the whole Church has rethought its understanding of the liturgy in the light of the new culture in which we must live, unless we are to die with the old. And that raises the real problem of cultural relativity.

The problem of cultural relativity lies in the fact that the faith is not tied to any one culture, even those which are largely its own creation, and yet that at no point do we possess the faith culturally nude. We are not able to make the faith our own at all except in a culture. We cannot simply strip the faith of the thought-forms, images and myths in which it has come to us, and then at our own will re-clothe it in fresh ones. Such a process, if it were possible, would presuppose that we had it in our power for a moment to grasp the faith apart from all cultural embodiment, completely 'demythologized', freed from all imagery and symbolism, freed from that whole analogical and linguistic element which it always has in our minds. We cannot do that while the Church is in its earthly pilgrimage: we shall only be able to do that when we see God face to face, and know even as we are known.

The cultural embodiment of the revelation is precisely the means by which it becomes real to our minds. Our task then is a subtle one, and there are no short-circuits, modernist or Bult-mannite. We can only perform our task of re-adaptation to new cultures if we remain authentically Christian, faithful to the Apostolic Tradition as it has come to us, and at the same time authentically members of our own culture. We must not be afraid to ask dangerous questions, as we take up the task of making the faith real to ourselves without adopting some alien culture in the process. The modernists, or liberals, were not wrong to ask their questions, though it now seems to the Church that they did not reach correct answers. In the same way, Rudolf Bultmann is not wrong to ask the question of whether it is possible to make the faith a live option for modern man by a radical 'demythologizing'. The question is rather whether in thus attacking the cultural problem of our time he is reaching answers which safeguard the authentic Apostolic Tradition.

If the answer to this question seems to many, including the present writer, to be 'No' this is not to blame Bultmann for try-ing. Bultmann, if we have understood him rightly, starts from the fact to which we have here drawn attention, that all cul-tural embodiments of the revelation are relative to the revelation itself. He does not, at least in intention (though perhaps in result), make the liberal mistake of abridging the Gospel, so that it is reduced to a mere glow of uplift upon the culture itself. Bultmann raises the question of whether the original cultural embodiment of the revelation is not even more relative than we have hitherto supposed. He suggests that we might altogether discard the mythological framework of Jewish and Hellenistic culture in which the revelation first found expression, and reinterpret it in terms of modern existentialism.

How far, then, is the first cultural embodiment of the revelation also relative? Can we demythologize it away, or must it be transmitted to every generation along with the revelation it embodies? The answer seems to the present writer to be that we cannot demythologize it away, not because it is not, as Bultmann supposes, relative, but for two somewhat different reasons. The first is that there is no intervening moment between one cultural embodiment of the revelation and the next, in which we could have the pure Gospel in our hands without any cultural embodiment at all. We only discover gradually what is not relative as we consider a number of different relative embodiments. Any expression of the revelation whatever will itself be relative to the living knowledge of God through Christ. The second reason is that the New Testament cultural embodiment of the Gospel, though relative, is not accidental. Bultmann seems to suppose that it does not matter at which point in history God became incarnate. He might as well not have been a Jew at all. Now this seems to be the error which the Church rejected in Marcion, the greatest of the early heretics. The incarnation of God cannot be separated from the preparatory revelation of God to Israel. Hebrew thought may well, therefore, have a special relationship to the Gospel, which we cannot sever. Our cultural translation will have to carry with it a certain amount of Hebrew thought, because at least part of Hebrew thought is itself the product of the impact of the acts of God on the Hebrew people.

On the other hand, the New Testament is itself evidence of

one very striking cultural transformation. In the later books of the New Testament, and perhaps to some extent in all of them, we find the faith rapidly being transplanted from a Hebrew to a Hellenistic environment, as the Church discovers that her witness will increasingly have to be made to a Gentile world. Although it seems to be the conclusion of the latest biblical scholarship that interaction between the Jewish and the Hellenistic worlds had already begun well before the writing of the New Testament, so that Hellenistic elements in the New Testament are not necessarily late, there can be no real doubt that the Apostolic Church found a work of translation necessary and set about it with the zest of true missionaries. The New Testament itself lays the foundations of the European form of Christianity.

It may be said, then, that the New Testament gives us authority to believe that cultural transplantation of the faith is possible, and also gives us a specimen of what happens when it is authentically done. We notice how in this transformation of the Hebraic idiom of faith the Greek idiom of thought and behaviour is also radically transformed by the impact of the revelation, and something new is created. Christianity in its Gentile form was after all very different from the Gnostic and Hermetic mystery cults which surrounded it, and it made converts from their adherents as much because it offered what they did not offer as because it could use a cultural expression not too unfamiliar to them. Part of the importance of the New Testament to the Church, and part of the reason for its normative position, lies in the fact that it gives us not only the original cultural clothing of the revelation, but also a second clothing of the revelation in another though not wholly unrelated culture.

From the New Testament we can observe just how much in the Hebraic form of Christianity the Apostolic Church thought essential to the faith, and therefore to be carried over into the Hellenistic translation. From the combination of these two embodiments, both represented in the New Testament, we can understand much better than from either alone the essence of the revelation itself, even if we cannot grasp it at all except in one or other of its cultural forms. Thus the New Testament can help us in our own task of translating the Gospel out of old European form into more than one new form. We have no advantage precisely corresponding to that which the Apostles had, of being able to draw upon a previous cultural adaptation of Judaism to the Hellenistic world, but to counterbalance that, the cultures with which the Church is concerned today are either descended from, or have recently been influenced by, the older European one, at least in its post-Renaissance form.[1]

Now, while the Apostolicity of the Church is connected with its capacity to remain faithful to the original revelation in history, and so also to the first cultural expression of it, its Catholicity is connected with its capacity to become indigenous in every new culture, not to be tied to any past cultural expression in such a way as to be unable to break loose. For Christianity is not, and must be seen not to be, simply the product of any human culture at all, even the Hebraic, considered merely from a human point of view. If Christianity is divine truth, then it belongs to all men, whatever their culture. Christianity needs very much to be vindicated from the suspicion that it is simply a part of the old European culture that is passing away in Europe and is in any case not for export to Asia and Africa.

Just because Christianity is revelation, it is not ultimately the religion of European man. Yet it is now, and has been, in part precisely that. If we distinguish Christianity, as an empirical religion, from the revelation of which it is the cultural embodiment, it must be regarded to a great extent as European man's religion, just because in Europe Christianity has been so successful in uniting itself with the prevalent culture. It is the past success of the Christian mission in Europe which is now jeopardizing its success in the culturally self-conscious countries of Asia, as well as in that modern Western culture which is so different from the older culture of Europe, to which we refer when we speak of Western values.

[1] For the foregoing see, e.g., Hoskyns and Davey, *The Riddle of the New Testament*.

The vitality and Catholicity of Christianity will show itself in its capacity to take root in every new cultural situation. If it does that authentically, then the Apostolic Tradition will be continually enriched by the contribution of men of many different cultures, as in each of them men learn to make the revelation real to themselves in the terms of their own culture. Each cultural embodiment of the one faith makes a permanent contribution to the whole heritage of the Church. Her Catholicity is a growing thing: it comes to its fullness only when every nation and culture is making its full contribution to the whole. We must therefore learn to envisage Christianity as much more vital and diverse than has hitherto been the case, as its life becomes enriched by those who have hitherto either made no contribution at all, or have found little opportunity to do so because they were expected to assimilate Western culture along with the faith. We need to have the Scriptures interpreted for us by men of Asia and Africa and Latin America, as well as by men of the new scientific culture of the 'Western' world.

If this is to happen, we must expect to find the question of the unity of the Church taking on new urgency. It is much more difficult for men to judge whether they are really one in the Church if they live as authentic members of very different cultures. That is part of the reason why so many Christian traditions insist on converts absorbing the culture of the missionary, as well as his faith. Only then can they be sure of them. But the lesson of the present demand for cultural liberation in the younger churches, notably in China, is that those days have passed. These churches must learn to be themselves, and to become missionaries to their own people. Those who have brought them the faith must stand back and let them make it real to themselves in their own way. If they do not stand back, they will be pushed back anyway by the pressure of events.

We must therefore welcome cultural diversity in the Church as a sign of vitality and true Catholicity. But cultural diversity involves theological diversity, as well as diversity in worship.

Diversity is a result of identification, as local churches take root in their own culture; but cultural identification carried too far means syncretism, compromising the revelation with the surrounding culture, and often with the non-Christian religion which has bound it together. Too great cultural diversity at the theological level means that the unity of the Church is threatened because men cannot recognize their own faith in other people's cultural forms. It may even mean the presence of heresy, because in the desire to be authentic members of their own culture churches have genuinely lost contact with the Apostolic Tradition. Here again we see how essential it is that the Apostolic Tradition should be controlled by a norm, which ensures the proper tension between Apostolicity and Catholicity, whereby each remains itself. If the Church needs the wisest possible Catholicity, which means the widest possible cultural diversity, for the full apprehension of the one revelation, for the richest possible interpretation of Scripture, it needs to retain the Scriptures always, as the norm for what is to be regarded as authentically apostolic.

The developing and spreading tradition of the Church means a continual enrichment of her capacity to interpret Scripture, and to develop doctrine according to the needs of every age and culture. Through such developments the Holy Spirit sheds ever fresh light on the one revelation, to the permanent advantage of the whole Church. Thus authentic tradition, beginning with the rule of faith, going on to the creeds, and including the theological developments of every cultural embodiment of the faith, is the proper and indispensable key to the understanding of Scripture. We cannot understand the Scriptures unless we live in the Church, with its first-hand knowledge of the faith, and with the breadth of its understanding of the implications of faith. To ignore the breadth of the tradition of the Church means becoming the prisoner of one's own culture. This is precisely what happens to the fundamentalist churches, who suppose that they can by-pass tradition and go direct to Scripture, but also in fact all unknowingly become terribly provincial and narrow in their interpretation of it, and in consequence very unfitted for the missionary role for which they cast themselves.

On the other hand, if tradition is the key to Scripture, Scripture is the norm of tradition. The canon of Scripture stands in the Church as the norm by which we can test all subsequent tradition, to distinguish the authentic stream from the perverted and heretical. No understanding of the revelation developed subsequently to Scripture can be necessary to salvation, or what is saying the same thing, an essential form of the unity of the Church. And no traditional development of doctrine which is inconsistent with Scripture can be genuinely apostolic. The normative role of Scripture is consequent upon the historical nature of the Christian revelation. The revelation was given in Jesus Christ, who lived at a certain point in time. He commissioned and authorized his own interpreters, who were guided by the Holy Spirit in the construction of the first and normative expression of the revelation. Holy Scripture is the record of the apostolic witness to the one revelation in Christ. It cannot therefore be altered or added to by subsequent generations in the Church.

Tradition on the other hand can never be closed until the return of Christ: it is an essential function of the Church's mission, of its spreading of the good news, 'to the ends of the earth and to the end of the world'. Wherever the Church is healthily spreading and over-passing new frontiers, tradition will be developing. But it can add nothing to the content of saving faith, which is contained in Scripture. Tradition is the product of the work of the Holy Spirit in the Church as the inward principle of reception of the objective revelation in Christ. But the Holy Spirit never says anything of his own. He says only what is Christ's and the Father's. He builds only upon the foundation of the historic revelation in the incarnate Christ, and since our knowledge of that history is contained entirely in Scripture, the sole role of tradition is to enrich our interpretation of Scripture. Thus Scripture and tradition have a delicate and reciprocal relationship. Each is necessary to the other. Jesus Christ, who is Lord both of Scripture and tradition, uses both through the Holy Spirit for the building up of his Church. He uses Scripture to correct the perversions to which free tradition would be subject, and tradition to prevent the misunderstandings of Scripture to which it would be exposed by an untraditional interpretation.

At this subtle point of the interaction and reciprocal control of Scripture and tradition lies the vocation of the theologian in the Church. The theologian, whoever he may be, priest or layman, specialist or occasional practitioner, is the one who finds it his special calling in the Church to express the revelation in thought. He offers his mind to Jesus Christ to be used by the Holy Spirit for the articulation of the Church's faith in his own time. His special task is to expound faithfully the original revelation in the idioms of the culture in which he lives. His primary loyalty, his own overriding one, is to the revelation itself, and his first duty is to understand it. The most basic proposition in Christian theology is that a revelation has taken place. It is this revelation which uniquely and decisively must govern the thought of the theologian. He must set forth 'the truth as it is in Christ', to speak of God as revealed in Christ, and so only. His discipline is 'to make every thought captive for Christ', to bring all his own thinking, and all the teaching for which he has any responsibility, into obedience to the one truth of revelation. Non-revelational theology is the greatest danger that faces the Church, for if her understanding of the basis of her own life goes astray, all else will in the end follow.

Thus the first task of the theologian is to study Scripture in the light of tradition. He must make his own as much as possible of the Church's heritage of understanding and expressing the one revelation in Christ. He is seeking not merely a historical analysis of what this or that writer thought, but the living faith of the Church, and in this search all the historical disciplines will be necessary, but they will be means to a greater end. It is a weakness of the Church in England, and to a lesser extent in the whole English-speaking world, that she lacks the discipline of dogmatic theology, which is the supreme business of the thought of a Church that knows itself bound to a revelation. If there is no revelation to govern our thought, we may well be content to study the Bible and the Fathers historically, or to interpret them as we choose in the light of the latest craze in philosophy. But where there is no provision for men to spend their whole time in learning the discipline of dogmatics, and in teaching it to others, the true theology that is done will be of an amateurish and irresponsible kind, or as very often happens, the natural and proper urge of the Christian theologian to do dogmatics will be satisfied indirectly and indeed illicitly by its importation as a form of bias into historical studies. Much so-called historical theology is cloaked dogmatics, and would be better done openly and under the proper disciplines of the subject, which are as rigorous as those of any other branch of theology. In none of the English universities is there a school or department of dogmatics, and no student can at present offer dogmatics, except in the historical sense, as an examination subject. The doctrine papers in the General Ordination Examination of the Church of England are no substitute for the absence of dogmatics as an academic discipline. The standard required is far too low, and the curriculum too narrowly conceived, for the need of the Church to be met.

The reason for this tragic gap in the intellectual life of the Church is not unconnected with the past sins of her members. If the universities were to be interrogated as to the reason for the absence of a school of dogmatics, their reply would probably be that they have no business with sectarian questions of this kind, but only with facts. They are not concerned with what the Church should believe, but with public facts such as can take their place in any history of ideas. If dogmatics were re-introduced into the curriculum, the churches would be at one another's throats. How should we reply? One reply would be that these matters are in practice decided by the faculties of divinity, that is by the university teachers of theology themselves, who are for the most part members, and indeed ministers, of Christian churches. It is not in every university that they are bound by statute to exclude these matters.

Where such exclusion of dogmatics is enforced by university statute, the Church may well have to repent and bide her time, knowing that the sectarian and party struggles of the past are the cause of the present ban. But where the members of the Church are themselves in control of what is taught and studied, the only possible conclusion is that they have forgotten that the supreme business of the theologian is with revelation, and that the historical studies lose all point if they are not the prolegomena to dogmatics. And to the university at large it may be said that the faith of the Christian Church is as important a matter for the study of those who wish to engage in it as the views of any philosopher, who is allowed today to teach his own system without let or hindrance. The theologian is at least as much concerned with truth, and with the rigorous discipline of adjusting his mind to the demands of the truth. Dogmatics has every reason to be regarded as a genuinely academic discipline in this country as it is on the continent of Europe.

It would, however, be a legitimate demand of the university, if it were made, that the dogmatic theologian should not confine himself to the teaching of his own church, but should be useful to members of other churches also. It would be the contention of the present writer that this demand can be met without the loss of any of the responsibility proper to the dogmatic theologian, who speaks for the Church and not simply for himself. The ecumenical movement has progressed to a point where no responsible teacher in any theological subject would think of confining his own reading, or that of his pupils, to books written by members of his own church. The impoverishment would be too great to contemplate. However convinced we may be of the rightness of the teaching of our own church, we regard it as essential to enrich it from the work of theologians of other traditions. There is a common pool of theology on which we all draw.

Thus it would be the task of the university teacher of Christian dogmatics, if such a person existed in England, to teach out of the common tradition of all the Churches, out of that great tradition which is older and broader (though not vaguer or less responsible) than any of them. This responsibility to go beyond the particular needs of his own church, and to teach an ecumenical dogmatics, would not preclude him from presenting the Christian faith, as every such teacher must, from his own personal standpoint, which would be governed very much by his church membership. But his pupils would know well enough how to use his teaching without compromising the faith of their own churches. It is well known already how the great teachers of dogmatics of our time inspire members of many different churches, without in any way detaching them from their proper allegiance. Indeed, ecumenical dogmatics already exists, and it would be well for our universities to become aware of the fact and to give opportunity for it to be studied in an academically adequate way. The time has passed when the undesirable consequences they fear would be likely to follow. The historical subjects as already taught in our faculties of divinity contain as explosive material as anything which would be taught in a department of dogmatic theology.

The need of the dogmatic theologian today to do his work in a wider context than the tradition of his own church is connected with his whole calling to interpret the revelation as recorded in Scripture in the context of tradition. It would be agreed by every church that not everything which is traditional in its own life is part of the Apostolic Tradition, and equally that elements of the Apostolic Tradition are to be found in the faith and life of other churches. It is often, and justly, remarked that the most important theological cleavages today run across and not along denominational boundaries. The theologian today is bound to do his work in an ecumenical context, whatever his discipline. He needs to do this precisely in order to understand as well as possible the one revealed truth of God in Christ. If we need tradition to help us to understand our faith in all its grandeur and breadth, then we need all tradition.

It is here, as we have seen, that the task of the theologian is also a critical one. He needs to expose all traditional interpretations of the faith to one another, lest he make an arbitrary selection from the tradition, and he needs to expose all that is tradition to the criticism of Scripture. And in doing all this, he needs to be a man of his time, without succumbing to the fashions of his time. He needs to live in his own culture, and indeed at its growing point, and not in some cultural ghetto of introverted ecclesiastical life. He must be trying to make the faith real to himself within the culture of his time and not outside it, and yet he must be continually exposing his conclusions to the test of a broader and older tradition and all these to Scripture itself. Theology is a discipline because it is not free speculation, but a critical study, imposed by the revelation itself. Theology seeks to bring the whole life of the Church under obedience to the revelation in Christ.

VII

The Revelation of God the Creator

IN revealing himself to his people in the act of redeeming them, God reveals himself also as the creator of the world. His people, like all other peoples, already knew of stories and myths of the creation, and some of these entered into their reflection upon the preparatory revelation, and were in turn modified by it. But they knew him as their creator because they had encountered him personally in history as their redeemer, that is, as the maker of a new creation. In thus experiencing his creative power they understood that he was the maker of the whole world. It is therefore untrue to say that the doctrine of creation must be for Christians a presupposition of the doctrine of redemption: on the contrary, in the order of faith, the doctrine of redemption is the presupposition of the doctrine of creation, and may even be said to include it. The full Christian doctrine of the creation depends upon the new creation, which, beginning in the womb of the Virgin Mary, is established finally at the resurrection, and into which we are incorporated in Baptism.

In revealing himself as the creator in his redemption of the world, God also vindicates himself against the great question set against him by the evil in the world. Redeemed man learns to look beyond the evil in the world to the almighty love of God: he sees the whole world as the place of God's glory, and from his own experience of his utter dependence on God's grace, learns to understand the dependence of all things on the creative Word of God. Christian faith is therefore able to develop a theology of the creation, of God's act in creating it, and of the creation as the sphere in which God is to be glorified by the Church. Christian philosophy, which claims the natural for God, is therefore also dependent, even when it does not realize it, upon God's revelation of himself.

If God makes himself known to man through the narrow
way of the flesh of Jesus Christ, he shows himself there as no
less than the creator of the universe. The God whom we meet
in Jesus is not concerned only with our weakness and alienation from him and from our true selves, but also with all our
potentialities of glorifying him as we live in his image in the
world which he has made for us. Thus our study of revelation
in Christ must end with the full sweep of the Christian faith in
God as the creator of the world. Only so, indeed, can we make
clear the truth of what has been said several times earlier, that
Christianity is not, in any ordinary sense of the word, a religion.
It does not or should not set up some special religious sphere
in which alone we have dealings with God, invoking him only
when we need him to supplement our weakness, but its sphere
is the whole of life, to be lived in the presence of God and in
dependence upon him, and therefore to his glory. It follows
again from this whole understanding of Christianity that Christ
restores the natural, that the Christian life is not so much the
supernatural life, but the truly natural, what Charles Williams
called the 'arch-natural'. Through Christ we enter into our
inheritance in the creation, and take up again our forfeited
dominion over it in him.

Our Christological understanding of revelation, which has
been the theme of this book, commits us, as it did the New
Testament writers, to a Christological view of creation. Christ
is the one 'by whom all things were made'. God the creator is
not to be thought of otherwise than in Christ. It is in and
through Christ who was incarnate in Palestine and died on a
cross that God made all things. The Father alone is not the
creator: he creates the world through the Son who is his Word
and his Wisdom. It follows that man cannot fully know his
creator until he reveals himself in Christ: the preparatory revelation of the Father in the history of Israel casts only a veiled
light upon God the creator. More than this, God first makes
himself known to man as redeemer, and man knows his God
as creator only through knowing him as redeemer.

All over the world we find stories of the creation of the

world as part of the 'natural' religion of fallen man. Such myths are also common to the religious world of the Near East, in which the people of the revelation lived. At the time when God first made himself known to Israel, in his calling of Moses and his redemption of the people from bondage in Egypt, the people were doubtless aware of such stories. At a later stage, when the people had settled in Palestine, and changed their way of life from the nomadic existence of the desert to the agricultural economy of Canaan, their religion seems to have entered a syncretistic phase, in which the LORD could be confused with and assimilated to the Baalim, the fertility gods of their Canaanite neighbours. Old Testament scholars, especially of the school of the cultic historians, see traces in the Psalms and elsewhere of a ritual whereby the LORD is annually enthroned as King, associated with the idea of the renewal of creation in the New Year.

In this phase, where the historical religion of the Exodus is in the background, the LORD becomes a Nature God, albeit a high God, and his role as creator is to continue to assure the fertility of nature. It is at this point that the prophets begin to recall the nation to the old religion of pre-Canaanite days, stressing again that the LORD is a jealous God, separating him off sharply from the neighbouring gods. The prophetic conception of God involves a purification of the creation stories, and the oldest biblical creation story, that associated with Genesis 2, already bears the marks of the prophetic religion. The essence of Mosaic and prophetic religion lies in God's choice of Israel and covenant with the people, manifested in his redemptive activity in the Exodus. He is not a Nature God, still less a tribal deity: if he has a specific role, it is as Lord of history. His relationship with Israel is not natural, it is dependent upon his own decision. He is not therefore simply the God of Israel, but the God of all the world.

When such a conception of God, derived from the preparatory revelation, plays upon the stock of myths and stories of the creation, they are bound to be transformed. We no longer find the typical ideas of God as the demiurge, the great artificer who works up the raw material of creation into shape, or as the god who assures the fertility of nature for man, whose worship is largely a magical propitiation of the foundation of the economy, but we move towards the Christian conception of the God who creates all things out of nothing. In all probability even the magnificent Priestly narrative of Genesis 1, unique among creation stories, does not quite reach the clear insight of the utter dependence of all things on God. There is still a trace of the mythical idea of the primeval chaos defeated by God and shaped into the world. In essence the Priestly narrative, which probably reached its final form, after long growth and fashioning in a continuous tradition, only during the Exile in Babylon, is the product of Mosaic and prophetic religion, of men who knew God in his mighty acts in history and in the power of his Word, who knew him as the one who had rescued them by his mighty hand from Egypt and had now in judgement swept them off into exile by his Word. And so these thinkers see God as creating the world in the same way, simply by his Word, his *fiat*. They know him as the only God, the creator of heaven and earth, because they have learned to know him as Lord of history, calling up what nations he will to mould the destiny of his people.

If the idea of God as creator first entered the minds of the men of Israel through the stories of creation that they, in common with other peoples, told, the final form of these stories, unique in all religious literature, is what it is because they have learned of God's true nature from his redeeming work in history, in calling, choosing and liberating his people. Creation is an extension of the covenant. Its orderliness, which takes them beyond magical propitiation, is the reflection of the faithfulness of God to his covenant promises which they have learned of in history. God is known as creator because he is known in history as the one who can bring strength out of weakness, who can bring something out of nothing, as when he made Israel a nation. Even under the Old Covenant God is partially revealed as creator, because he is already partially known as redeemer.

All this finds its fulfilment and perfection in the New Covenant. The author of the New Creation is there seen fully to be the author of the Old, and as the experience of redemption is profoundly intensified, so creation is more sharply apprehended. For the first time, man can fully understand creation as *ex nihilo, ex ouk onton*, not even *ek me onton*; creation depends for its existence, and not merely for its form, upon the Creator. There is not even a potentiality of existence, a non-being striving towards being, out of which God may make the world. And this is but the analogue of the total dependence of redeemed man upon grace. If man contributes nothing to his own redemption, creation owes its existence also to the utter generosity of the Creator. Creation itself is seen as an act of grace.

God reveals himself as creator in Christ, for he there acts to regenerate man who is dead in sin, as he raises Christ from the dead. The resurrection, and the regeneration of man in the Body of the resurrected, are supremely the *act* of God the creator. Man who has experienced that almighty act can never again think of the world as simply in a state of being: he will see it as having been brought into being by an act, as his own new life has been. Man who has experienced the regenerative power of the Word of God in the gospel of Christ will read the Genesis stories with new eyes, and recognize in the Word that brought the world into being and order the same Word that has spoken to him in Christ. Thus, as the power of God in redemption throws light on the profundity of the idea of creation, the thought of creation plays back again upon redemption, as men reflect upon it, and see in it the guarantee of the perfection of the new creation at the end of the world. 'Behold, I make all things new.' The final consummation of redemption is a new heaven and a new earth as the dwelling place of the redeemed community. Again, the might of God in the resurrection and the re-creation of believers is seen as continuing the creative act: 'God chose what is low and despised in the world, even the things that are not, to bring to nothing things that are, so that no human being might boast in the presence of the Lord. He is the source of your life in Christ Jesus. . . .' (I Cor. 1.28-30.)

It is therefore at best a half-truth to say that for Christian theology the doctrine of redemption needs as its presupposition the doctrine of creation. It is, indeed, true that the New Testament writers know of a doctrine of creation, based upon the reflection of their Old Testament predecessors upon the preparatory revelation, itself a redemptive act, so that they can interpret the redemption as a new creation. But the doctrine of creation itself is so deepened in meaning by the light cast upon it in Christ as to become a new doctrine, now taken utterly out of the realm of myth. The old biblical stories are still used, but they are filled with a content derived from Christ. Later Christian reflection will develop a doctrine of creation that owes more to the final revelation in Christ than to its preparation in the Old Testament. If the Christian doctrine of creation is unique, it is because it derives from the unique revelation of God in Christ. It would therefore be better to say that in the order of faith we always come to know God first in those actions, which are always redeeming ones, in which he comes to meet us in history.

For the Christian this means that we know God, as this book has throughout sought to make clear, first of all in Christ. In finding God there we discover the one who is also the creator of the whole world. Thus we may say either that in his revelation of himself through redemption God shows himself to be the Creator, which is to say that the doctrine of redemption includes the doctrine of creation, so far as our reflection upon the historic revelation is concerned. Or we may say, putting it more strikingly still and yet without straining language too much, that the doctrine of redemption is actually the presupposition for the doctrine of creation; since this was quite certainly so for the men of the Old Testament, it may easily be the case for Christians now.

For while the Church inherited from Israel old myths and speculations about creation, reworked in the light of the preparatory revelation in history so that they became the Word of

God, truly teaching a faith in him as creator, the Church had in sober fact what Israel had only in analogy, the experience of God's creative power. The Church knew of the work of God in the new creation, beginning in the womb of the Virgin Mary, continuing in the raising of Christ from the dead in all his physical reality, and consummated in the Church as the spreading of the new creation throughout humanity. Baptismal regeneration brings man into personal contact with God in his creative work. For in all these events there is discontinuity, new beginning, as well as continuity with what had gone before. The virginal conception of Jesus is an act of new creation, for though he is nourished in the womb of his mother, and is born as all other men are born, the starting point of the human life of Jesus is not the coming together of two earthly parents, but the act of the Holy Spirit in bringing into being what was not there before.

The resurrection is again a new creation: there is no natural immortality, according to the biblical faith: Jesus does not 'survive' death, he is raised from the dead by the mighty power of God, even if we must go on to say that this is because he 'could not be holden of' death, and that he regains for man a destiny of eternal life which was part of God's original plan. And the new creation of spiritual life, which occurs when men are born again at Baptism into the Body of Christ, is again genuine creation, even though it builds upon the existence of the fallen sinner who is brought to new life.

Thus the Church could work back from her daily experience of the new creation to the beginning of all things, and see that as God was now re-creating humanity in Jesus, so he had made the world in him in the beginning. The prologue to the Fourth Gospel reaches this final point when it says that all things were made by the Word, that is by the one who is preached to us as Saviour. And if the doctrine of redemption is thus the presupposition of the doctrine of creation, if creation is read back from redemption, this is certainly not to minimize the importance of the creation in Christian faith. Just the contrary. In this perspective creation is revealed as not so much the presupposition as the end and object of redemption. The crown of God's redemptive work is the new creation, in which the New Adam has all things set under his feet, and man in Christ is God's vice-gerent over the creation, controlling it all to the glory of God. This perspective takes us out of any pietistic notion of the unnaturalness of the redeemed life, and set us securely in the sphere of the truly natural, as revealed in Christ. Christ is the consummation of all things, both in heaven and in earth.

Twentieth-century man also knows of stories of creation, and very often, since his acquaintance with mature Christian teaching may be slight, he regards the Christian view of creation as being one more nature myth. He sees the Christian view of God as a speculative way of accounting for the world, and rejects it because of the evil in the world. The humanist today rejects the view that there is a loving God who made the world, because it seems to him inconsistent with the suffering of the innocent, the pain in the world, and nature red in tooth and claw. The problem of evil is brought before us in a dilemma, as old as St Augustine, but having lost nothing of its searching power. Either God can stop this evil and he will not, in which case he is not good. Or he would like to stop it and he cannot, in which case he is not almighty. Whichever horn of the dilemma we opt for, any credible view of God has been dealt a mortal blow. And if we say that the evil is not really as bad as it looks, that only sin is really evil, and God has taken measures to stop that, then we are told that we are bringing forward a view of God that offends man's moral sense. We cannot believe in a God who is less compassionate than ourselves.

Against such a counter-apologetic, no doctrine of the creation which is not securely anchored in the Christological revelation can live. The problem of evil is no dialectical trick, put forward irresponsibly as a mere debating point. If we treat it in that way, we merely show the superficiality of our own theology, and deserve to lose, as we always shall if we argue with unbelievers in these terms, and with such contempt for their honesty and integrity. On the contrary, the problem of evil is an acid solvent, which leaves nothing behind of a merely metaphysical or speculative doctrine of the creation. If we suppose that we can build our edifice of Christian doctrine on the foundation of a natural theology of the creation, we shall merely display our incapacity to think in realities, and show ourselves playing with ideas and unable to meet the men of our time. Only God's historic revelation of himself in Christ crucified and risen can vindicate him as the loving creator of the world in which evil is thus a problem.

There is, indeed, no speculative theory which we can put forward as the answer to the problem of evil. Even the traditional Christian apologetic based upon the impossibility of God taking away the freedom that he has given to his creation founders on the rock of the twofold meaninglessness of a definition of freedom, in terms of ability to do evil, which robs God himself of freedom, and is in any case inapplicable to the lower creation in which so much of the evil which distresses us resides. Only mythology can attribute cancer to freedom and its misuse. And as Professor Flew has pointed out,[1] it is not irrational to conceive of a world in which freedom did not lead to evil. Indeed, the evil in the world is more than a problem, it is a challenging mystery, which can only be adequately met by the mystery of the suffering love of God crucified by those he came to save.

It is in Jesus who died in agony upon the Cross, the supremely innocent sufferer, that we see the real depth of the problem of evil, and also its mysterious resolution. The most evil thing that ever happened was the betrayal, condemnation and death of Jesus. There if anywhere we see the revolt of evil against good, its blind irrational desire to destroy and pull down into nothingness all that is of God, all that is kind and compassionate, all that is strong and splendid. And we see also, in the human sense, the invariable success of evil. It is just there, at its typical, even its strongest point, that God meets evil with something stronger than itself. The suffering

[1] *New Essays in Philosophical Theology*, pp. 149ff.

of the innocent is transformed in meaning by being voluntarily undertaken on behalf of the guilty. The utmost reach of evil serves only to call out the greater love of God. God accepts responsibility for the world he has made, and himself in the darkness and agony of the human nature he has taken upon himself suffers the evil of his creation, in order that he may have the right unequivocally to pronounce it good. The worst thing that ever happened becomes the occasion of the best. The whole power of the onslaught of evil is converted by the love of Christ into the strength in which the world is redeemed. Thus as we enter in the Church into the most intimate identification with Christ who died, no evil can separate us from the love of God. And the resurrection, which is the sign of the victory over evil which Christ won on the Cross, is the foretaste of the new heaven and the new earth in which evil will be no more. We cannot dare to condemn God for making a world in which the evil of men's hatred of goodness calls out such majesty of love. In the Cross, the supreme moment of revelation, God vindicates himself against the charge of non-existence, and his world as good.

God does not offer us in his revelation of himself on the Cross a new theory of the world, which will discount the facts alleged against it by those who draw attention to its evil. The facts remain what they are. But against them God sets something so great that they can no longer pull down the balance against God and his creation. His own love entering the darkest place of evil is disclosed as almighty. The light shone in the darkness, and the darkness did not overcome it. And when love has done its work in this world, God promises that 'all manner of thing shall be well.'

And so redeemed man, who has seen the glory of God in the face of Jesus Christ, who has seen a love so great that in it he can bear all the evil he cannot understand, goes joyfully forward into the world he now knows as God's, and there he can see God's glory. All men, even without revelation, can see a glory in the world. The beauty of nature and of human thought and goodness, the glory of the creative work of man in the arts and sciences, these need no revelation to disclose them. And many have seen in them sufficient argument for the existence of God. But once we have also seen the evil in the world, it becomes terribly hard to say Yes to it, in spite of the glory it contains. The glory of the world no longer evidences the creator—it becomes just one more inexplicable mystery. Revelation vindicates that glory as God's, and shows the believer new glories that before he was too blind to see. Having seen the love of God in Christ, he learns to recognize it again in the world.

The revelation on the Cross of God the creator means that there is nowhere in the world where God's glory may not be manifested, and nothing that ultimately can serve as an argument against God. That is why the believer, as he re-enters God's world, is unshakeable in his conviction that behind everything that happens is the love of God. No horror will move him from his faith, though humanly it may totter, for nothing can be worse than the Cross. If he is asked, as his humanist friends will ask him, what happening could conceivably make him give up his faith in the goodness and love of God, he is bound to reply that no such event can be conceived. Even where he cannot understand, he will, God helping him, continue to praise.

Thus, too, in the experience of grace, the believer knows fully the ontological dependence of the world on God. As he himself hangs over the void, supported only by the swinging rope of grace, he understands that all things else along with him are held in being by the love of God. Beside God, all that has been made is as nothing. If God withdrew his attention from it for a moment, it would lapse into the nothingness from which God called it. As man lives *sola gratia*, by grace alone, so the whole world and all that exists apart from God has its being from him *ex nihilo*, out of nothingness. Man's total dependence on grace, through redemption, is the sign of his total dependence on the creative love of God, for his whole being. Man's true being is to know his dependence, and accepting life from God in every moment, to praise him for it.

147

Thus man's response to revelation, his praise and thanksgiving of God, is made in the creation. Once God has revealed the world as his own, no lesser sphere will do for the response of man to God. Man, restored in Christ to his true being, made natural at last, will not be content to come to God only in some delimited sphere of the sacred. He will find the love of God, and therefore an opportunity to praise God, everywhere. Since his worship of God is not some humanly chosen religious way, which comes to God for those purposes and to meet those needs which man decides upon, with the result that God is excluded from the rest of life, but rather man's response to God's own gracious approach to him, man must respond to God wherever God chooses to be. God calls different men in different ways. He does indeed call some men to the specifically 'religious' way, to serve him in worship and in prayer, and to abstain from the work of the world. But even these 'religious', in the technical sense, need not, and ought not to, practise Christianity as a religion like the other religions. Indeed, for them above all, life as a whole is to be lived in the presence of God. Their life is no withdrawal from the secular into the sacred, if it is rightly understood, but a pressing forward into the eschatological life, to the world where all distinction between prayer and action breaks down, and both are one in the praise of God.

As the Church reflects upon the revelation of God the creator, she develops a theology of creation which grows out of her theology of redemption as its corollary. In practice, the order of faith is seldom adhered to, and almost all systematic expositions of the Christian faith deal with creation before redemption. Yet just as it is impossible even to expound the most basic Christian doctrine of all, that of revelation, without saying a great deal about the content of Christian faith, and especially the doctrines of the Trinity, the Incarnation, the Atonement and the Church, so it is impossible in a well-founded theology of the creation to avoid continual anticipation of what will be said under the heading of the doctrine of redemption. And if this anticipation is not made, if the theology of creation appears under the guise of philosophical speculation, then the disturbing influence of the revelation which lies in the background will manifest itself in the shape of formal invalidity in the argument.

This is surely the case with the whole magnificent mediaeval achievement in Christian philosophy. If this philosophy attempted to start from 'reason' alone and analyse the onto-logical dependence of the creation on God, and so reason from the contingency of the known world to the creator himself, the profundity and splendour its achievement was made possible only by the presence of the revealed knowledge of God at the very foundation of the thinking of these men. That is why, in spite of the fact that a more critical age detects the formal invalidity of the majority of their arguments, the Church will not soon abandon the work of the mediaeval thinkers. If their work, considered as philosophy, is no longer acceptable, if it no longer provides a bridge from the assump-tions of all educated men to the revealed faith of the Church, it may have a long life in its proper role, not as natural theo-logy, but as the theology of the natural.

Ontology has been heavily criticized by present-day theolo-gians, so much so that it has seemed that we were to be asked to accept existentialism as the new natural theology. It would be the contention of the present writer that existentialism is every bit as dangerous to theology as essentialist metaphysics, if it appears in the role of natural theology. But a theology that seeks to depend wholly upon revelation, which means a theology for which the concrete historical figure of Jesus Christ is always the centre and touchstone, will find in the revelation of God the creator the basis of an analysis of the dependence of the creation on God that may well find the terms of ontology the most appropriate for its purpose. As the Church in the light of revelation claims the whole world for God, there is still scope for a Christian philosophy that will not be content merely with its primary role of examining the logic of Chris-tian thinking, but will go on to relate this world to the God whose creation it is.

Whether in the end such a philosophy will be metaphysical or not will depend upon developments in the autonomous discipline of philosophy, over which the Church has no control, and should seek none. Since the Christian faith depends in no degree upon philosophy, except in so far as philosophy helps us to understand it, we can be content to let these events take their course. But Christians will have their part to play in such developments, for even though the Christian faith does not depend upon philosophy, it will not be indifferent to it. If our faith in God sends us into the world, we must move among the philosophers, though we are not in the last resort philosophers ourselves. The Christian philosopher can serve God in perfect freedom, following the truth where it leads him, for his faith is not in question, however far he may go in the critical scepticisms of this or any other age. He must fear the idol more than the inconoclast. God is not served by the billowing systems of the idealist, nor by the ruthlessness of the realist. But God is served by all striving after the truth, by all disciplines which detach men from self-interested prejudice, by all humble sitting down before the facts. These things do not save a man, but they make him less closed to the revelation when it comes to him. None the less, if a man believes, he knows well that it was by the grace of God alone, as his mind was illuminated to the truth as it is in Jesus by the grace of the Holy Spirit. And so to God alone he will give the praise.

Index

Index